Joseph Cook

Transcendentalism

Joseph Cook

Transcendentalism

ISBN/EAN: 9783337189457

Printed in Europe, USA, Canada, Australia, Japan

Cover: Foto ©Thomas Meinert / pixelio.de

More available books at **www.hansebooks.com**

Boston Monday Lectures.

TRANSCENDENTALISM,

WITH

PRELUDES ON CURRENT EVENTS.

By JOSEPH COOK.

"They who reject the testimony of the self-evident truths will find nothing surer on which to build." — ARISTOTLE.

BOSTON:
JAMES R. OSGOOD AND COMPANY.
(LATE TICKNOR & FIELDS, AND FIELDS, OSGOOD, & Co.)
1878.

INTRODUCTION.

THE object of the Boston Monday Lectures is to present the results of the freshest German, English, and American scholarship on the more important and difficult topics concerning the relation of Religion and Science.

They were begun in the Meionaon in 1875; and the audiences, gathered at noon on Mondays, were of such size as to need to be transferred to Park-street Church in October, 1876, and thence to Tremont Temple, which was often more than full during the winter of 1876–77.

The audiences contained large numbers of ministers, teachers, and other educated men.

The thirty-five lectures of the last season were stenographically reported in the Boston Daily Advertiser, and most of them were republished in full in New York and London.

The lectures on Biology oppose the materialistic, and not the theistic, theory of Evolution.

The lectures on Transcendentalism contain a discussion of the views of Theodore Parker.

The Committee having charge of the Boston Monday Lectures for the coming year consists of the following gentlemen: —

His Excellency A. H. RICE, Governor of Massachusetts.
Hon. ALPHEUS HARDY.
Hon. WILLIAM CLAFLIN, Ex-Governor of Massachusetts.
Prof. E. P. GOULD, Newton Theological Institute.
Rev. J. L. WITHROW, D.D.
REUBEN CROOKE.
Rev. WILLIAM M. BAKER, D.D.
RUSSELL STURGIS, Jr.
E. M. McPHERSON.

Prof. EDWARDS A. PARK, LL.D., Andover Theological Seminary.
Right Rev. BISHOP FOSTER.
Prof. L. T. TOWNSEND, Boston University.
ROBERT GILCHRIST.
SAMUEL JOHNSON.
Rev. Z. GRAY, D.D., Episcopal Theological School, Cambridge.
WILLIAM B. MERRILL.
M. H. SARGENT.
M. R. DEMING, *Secretary.*

BOSTON, September, 1877.

HENRY F. DURANT, *Chairman.*

PUBLISHERS' NOTE.

IN the careful reports of Mr. Cook's Lectures printed in the Boston Daily Advertiser, were included by the stenographer sundry expressions (applause, &c.) indicating the immediate and varying impressions with which the Lectures were received. Though these reports have been thoroughly revised by the author, the publishers have thought it advisable to retain these expressions. Mr. Cook's audiences included, in large numbers, representatives of the broadest scholarship, the profoundest philosophy, the acutest scientific research, and generally of the finest intellectual culture, of Boston and New England; and it has seemed admissible to allow the larger assembly to which these Lectures are now addressed to know how they were received by such audiences as those to which they were originally delivered.

CONTENTS.

LECTURES.

		PAGE
I.	INTUITION, INSTINCT, EXPERIMENT, SYLLOGISM, AS TESTS OF TRUTH	1
II.	TRANSCENDENTALISM IN NEW ENGLAND	27
III.	THEODORE PARKER'S ABSOLUTE RELIGION	53
IV.	CARICATURED DEFINITIONS IN RELIGIOUS SCIENCE	83
V.	THEODORE PARKER ON THE GUILT OF SIN	109
VI.	FINAL PERMANENCE OF MORAL CHARACTER	135
VII.	CAN A PERFECT BEING PERMIT EVIL?	165
VIII.	THE RELIGION REQUIRED BY THE NATURE OF THINGS	191
IX.	THEODORE PARKER ON COMMUNION WITH GOD AS PERSONAL	219
X.	THE TRINITY AND TRITHEISM	247
XI.	FRAGMENTARINESS OF OUTLOOK UPON THE DIVINE NATURE	277

PRELUDES.

		PAGE
I.	THE CHILDREN OF THE PERISHING POOR	3
II.	THE FAILURE OF STRAUSS'S MYTHICAL THEORY	29
III.	CHALMERS'S REMEDY FOR THE EVILS OF CITIES	55
IV.	MEXICANIZED POLITICS	85
V.	YALE, HARVARD, AND BOSTON	111
VI.	THE RIGHT DIRECTION OF THE RELIGIOUSLY IRRESOLUTE	137
VII.	RELIGIOUS CONVERSATION	167
VIII.	GEORGE WHITEFIELD IN BOSTON	193
IX.	CIRCE'S CUP IN CITIES	221
X.	CIVIL SERVICE REFORM	249
XI.	PLYMOUTH ROCK AS THE CORNER-STONE OF A FACTORY	279

I.

INTUITION, INSTINCT, EXPERIMENT, SYLLOGISM, AS TESTS OF TRUTH.

THE FIFTY-NINTH LECTURE IN THE BOSTON MONDAY LECTURESHIP, DELIVERED IN TREMONT TEMPLE, JAN. L

"HE would be thought void of common sense who asked on the one side, or, on the other, went to give, a reason why it is impossible for the same thing to be and not to be." — LOCKE: *Essay*, Book i. chap. iii.

"THERE is here a confession, the importance of which has been observed neither by Locke nor his antagonists. In thus appealing to common sense or intellect, he was in fact surrendering his thesis, that all our knowledge is an educt from experience. For in admitting, as he here virtually does, that experience must ultimately ground its procedure on the laws of intellect, he admits that intellect contains principles of judgment, on which experience being dependent, cannot possibly be their precursor or their cause. What Locke here calls common sense he elsewhere denominates intuition." — SIR WILLIAM HAMILTON: *Reid's Collected Writings*, vol. ii. p. 784.

TRANSCENDENTALISM.

I.

INTUITION, INSTINCT, EXPERIMENT, SYLLOGISM, AS TESTS OF TRUTH.

PRELUDE ON CURRENT EVENTS.

UNLESS the children of the dangerous and perishing classes are to blame for being born, they, at least, whatever we say of their parents, cannot be shut out from a victorious place in our pity. This is a festal day; and, if the Author of Christianity were on the groaning earth to make calls, probably the most of them, in the cities of the world, would be in unfashionable places. Why should we be so shy of the visitation in person of death-traps and rookeries? There is ineffable authority and example for going from house to house doing good. Visits thus enjoined cannot be made by proxy. No doubt organized and unorganized charity is usually, in its modern form, a result of the Christian spirit. Celsus said Christianity could not be divine, because it cared insanely for the poor. Old Rome's mood toward the miserable the world of culture now loathes. Philanthropy swells the tide of commiseration for the unfortunate; and sometimes the most erratic opinions have been conjoined with the soundest behavior toward those who have hardly where to lay their heads. Orthodoxy itself is often shy of personal contact with the very wretched, and goes from house to house by proxy. Organized charity, we think, is the whole of our duty. But Thomas Guthrie, and Dr. Chalmers, and all who have had much to do with the perishing classes in great cities, have taught the Church, that, when men are sick and in prison, they are to be visited. I know a great orator in this city, whose name is a power from sea to sea, and whose silvering honored head often bends over couch and cradle in the most miserable houses. It is safe to go to the North End now: it is not safe in the fiercest heats of summer.

Our North winds in winter strike us all the way from Boothia Felix, and their iciness seals some fever-dens, whose doors swing wide open every summer under the guardianship, as one must suppose, of the negligence of the Board of Health. [Applause.] I am not speaking at random; for, according to the city reports, there were in 1876 sixty-eight houses condemned as not conforming to the sanitary regulations of this city; and of these only seventeen were really vacated; the rest were white-washed. [Applause.] The truth is, that if there were ten Boards of Health, and if they all did their duty, we could not avoid having a large population born into the world miserable.

This nation now has one-fifth of its population in

cities. What are we to do with the social barriers which allow a great city to be not only a great world, but ten great worlds, in which one world does not care at all for what the other worlds are doing?

In every great town there are six or ten strata in society; and it is, one would think, a hundred miles from the fashionable to the unfashionable side of a single brick in a wall. Superfluity and squalor know absolutely nothing of each other — such is the utter negligence of the duty of visiting the poor, in any other way than by agents. I do not undervalue these, nor any part of the great charities of our times; but there is no complete theory for the permanent relief of the poor without personal visitation. Go from street to street with the city missionary or the best of the police; but sometimes go all alone, and with your own eyes see the poor in the attics, and study the absolutely unspeakable conditions of their daily lives. Not long ago, I was in a suffocated tenement-house where five or six points on which I could put my hand were in boldest violation of the laws which it is the business of the Board of Health in this city to see executed. [Applause.] The death-rate of Boston in summer, in the North End, is often above thirty-five in the thousand. The registrar-general of England says that any deaths above seventeen in a thousand are unnecessary. Live one day where the children of the perishing poor live, and ask what it is to live there always. I know a scholar of heroic temper and of exquisite culture, who recently resolved to live with the poor in a stifling part of this city, and who, after repeated and desperate illness, was obliged to move his home off the ground in order to avoid the necessity of putting his body underground. You cannot understand the poor by newspapers, nor even by novels.

Our distant lavender touches of the miserable show the barbaric blood yet in our veins. Going about from house to house doing good is a great Christian measure permanently instituted by a typical example, which in a better age may be remembered, and be the foundation of a nobility not yet visible on the planet. There was One who washed his disciples' feet, and in that act founded an order of nobility; but this second symbolic act seems not to be apprehended even yet by some good Samaritans — in gloves. The way from Jerusalem to Jericho lies now through the city slums; and, for many an age to come, there will be the spot where men oftenest will be left stripped and sore and half dead. We want all good influences of the parlor and press, from literature and the interior church of the church, to work upon the problem of saving the perishing and dangerous classes in great cities. [Applause.]

> Poor naked wretches, whereso'er you are,
> That bide the pelting of this pitiless storm,
> How shall your houseless heads and unfed sides,
> Your looped and windowed raggedness, defend you
> From seasons such as this? Take physic, pomp;
> Expose thyself to feel what wretches feel,
> That thou mayst shake the superflux to them,
> And show the heavens more just.
> LEAR, act iii. sc. iv.

[Applause].

TESTS OF TRUTH.

THE LECTURE.

Napoleon I., one day riding in advance of his army, came to a bridgeless river, which it was necessary that his hosts should immediately cross on a forced march. "Tell me," said the great emperor to his engineer, " the breadth of this stream."—" Sire, I cannot," was the reply. "My scientific instruments are with the army; and we are ten miles ahead of it." — " Measure the breadth of this stream instantly." — "Sire, be reasonable."—" Ascertain at once the width of this river, or you shall be deposed from your office." The engineer drew down the cap-piece on his helmet till the edge of it just touched the opposite bank; and then, holding himself erect, turned upon his heel, and noticed where the cap-piece touched the bank on which he stood. He then paced the distance from his position to the latter point, and turned to the emperor saying, " This is the breadth of the stream approximately;" and he was promoted. Now, in all the marches of thought, metaphysical science measures the breadth of streams with scientific instruments, indeed; but it uses no principles which men of common sense, at their firesides, or in politics, or before juries, or in business, do not recognize as authoritative. Your Napoleon's engineer, after his instruments came up, no doubt made a more accurate measurement than he had done by his skilful expedient of common sense; but the new and exact determination of the distance must have proceeded upon precisely the same principle by which he had made his approximate calculation. Both the estimates would turn on the scientific certainty that the radii of a circle are equal. The distance to the opposite bank is one radius in a circle, of which the position of the observer is the centre; and, if now he wheels round the radius, of course the radius here is just as long as the radius yonder; for things which are equal to the same thing are equal to each other. The most exact instruments ever invented would have behind them only that incontrovertible, axiomatic, self-evident truth. You can measure a river in the way Napoleon's engineer did; but you think that research of the metaphysical sort has something in it incomprehensible, mystical, and suspicious. Let us not stand in too much awe of the theodolite. As the engineer's final measurement of the river with scientific instruments was simply his pacing made exact, so metaphysics is simply common sense made exact.

After three months on Evolution, Materialism, and Immortality, the current of discussion in this Lectureship enters on a new vista; but the river is the same, for it flows out of that tropical land of Biology we have been traversing together, and the chief theme is always the relations of religion and science. It will yet be our duty to meditate on the application of the principle of evolution to philosophy, and especially to ethics; for I am now bidding adieu to Materialism as a topic, and am approaching Transcendentalism, and so Conscience, and so the natural conditions of the peace of the soul with itself and with the plan which inheres in the nature of things; that is, with God.

Here, as everywhere, religious science, like every other science, asks you to grant nothing but axiomatic truth. In considering Transcendentalism, or axiomatic tests of certainty, I must seem, therefore, to be almost transcendentalistic at first; for such is and must be all sound thought, up to a certain point. I am no pantheist; I am no individualist; I am no mere theist, I hope: but so far forth as Transcendentalism founds itself upon what Aristotle and Kant and Hamilton have called intuition, self-evident truths, axioms, first principles, I am willing to call myself a transcendentalist, not of the rationalistic, but of the Kantian, Hamiltonian, and Coleridgian school.

Both wings of the army front of Transcendentalism must be studied, and it will be found that it is only the left or rationalistic wing that has been of late thrown into panic. That serried and scattered and very brave host made bold marches in Boston thirty years ago. Its leaders now confess that it has been substantially defeated. *It is time for the right wing and centre to move.* This portion of Transcendentalism never broke with Christianity: the other portion did; and to-day, according to its own admission, is not only not victorious, but dispirited (Frothingham, Transcendentalism in New England, *passim*). Its historians speak of it as a thing of the past. Self-evident truths, axioms, necessary beliefs, however, can never go out of fashion; they can be opposed only by being assumed; they are a dateless and eternal noon.

Mr. Emerson's theoretical tests of truth are the intuitions or axioms of the soul, and undoubtedly these are the tests which the acutest philosophical science of the world now justifies, and has always justified. Whether the tests themselves justify pantheism, whether they give countenance to individualism like Mr. Emerson's, whether they establish mere theism, are grave and great questions that cannot be discussed here and now, but which we shall reach at the proper time. The whole of metaphysics, the whole philosophy of evolution, the whole of materialism, the whole of every thing that calls itself scientific, must submit itself to certain first truths; and therefore, on these first truths we must fasten the microscope with all the eagerness of those who wish to feel beneath them, somewhere in the yeasting foam of modern speculation, a deck that is tremorless.

What is an intuition?

Theodore Parker held that we have an "instinctive intuition" of the Divine Existence, and of immortality, and of the authority of the moral law. He constantly assumed that these facts are intuitive or self-evident, and as incontrovertible as the proposition that every change must have an adequate cause. He used the word "intuition" carelessly, and did not carefully distinguish *intuition* and *instinct* from each other. Very often, in otherwise brilliant literature, this vacillating and obscure use of the word "intuition" leads to most mischievous confusion of thought. We are told that woman's intuitions are better in many respects than man's; we are assured that the intuitions of childhood are purer, clearer, or more nearly unadulterated, than those of middle life: in short, our popular, and many of our scientific discussions, so far as these proceed from persons who have had no distinctively metaphysical training, use the word "intuition" with the most bewildering looseness. Individualism is justified by intuition; pantheism, mere theism, orthodoxy, or whatever a man feels, or seems to feel, to be true, he says his intuitions affirm. There are those who confuse intuition, not only with instinct, but with mere insight; that is, with an imaginative or reflective swiftness or emotional force, which, by glancing at truth, catches its outlines better than by laborious plodding. The loftiest arrogance of individualism justifies itself often simply by calling its idiosyncrasies intuitions. In all ages mysticism of the devoutest school has frequently made the same wild mistake. Gleams of radiance across the inner heavens of the great poetic souls of the race we must reverence; but shooting-stars are not to be confounded with the eternally fixed constellations. Undoubtedly a single flash of lightning from the swart, thunderous summer midnight, often ingrains the memory of a landscape more durably on the memory than the beating of many summer noons; but even lightning glances are not intuitions.

Our first business then, my friends, will be to obtain a distinct definition of the strategic word "intuition." This is a scientific technical term; and, when correctly used as such, has outlines as clearly cut as those of a crystal.

We must approach the definition in a way that will carry all minds with us, step by step.

1. It is possible to imagine all the *articles* in this room to be annihilated, or not in existence.

You feel very sure, do you not, as you cast a glance on the capacities of your mind, that you can believe that these articles *might* never have existed; and so of all other objects that fill space? Orion flames in our skies now; but you can at least imagine that this constellation might never have been. The Seven Stars we can suppose to be annihilated. I do not mean that we can prove matter to be destructible, but that we can imagine its non-existence. You are entirely certain of your mental capacity to imagine the non-existence of any material object in any part of space.

2. It is impossible to imagine the *space* in this room to be annihilated, or not in existence.

Notice the strange fact that you cannot so much as imagine the annihilation of a corner of the space in this room. You bring down in thought the space from one corner, as you would roll up a thick curtain; but you have left space behind, up yonder in the corner. You lift up this floor and bring down the ceiling: but you have left space beneath and above. You draw in all four sides of this temple at once, and cause its dimensions to diminish equally in every direction; but in every direction you have left space. If you go out into infinite space with the best exorcism of your magic, if you whip it as Xerxes whipped the ocean, you will find your heaviest lashes as unavailing as his. No part of space can even be imagined not to be in existence. We cannot so much as imagine that the space through which Orion and the Seven Stars wander should not be; by no possibility can you in thought get rid of it, although you easily get rid of them. That is a very curious fact in the mind.

3. It is possible to suppose all the *events* since sunrise not to have taken place.

I know not but that at this moment the English fleet lately in the Bosphorus is floating across the purple ripples of the Piræus harbor at Athens, in sight of the Acropolis. It may be that the Russians are commencing a march upon Turkey. But whatever has happened since sunrise I can imagine not to have happened at all. It is perfectly easy for me, in thought, to vacate all time of all events. Any thing that has taken place in time may be imagined not to have taken place. We can imagine the nonexistence of whatever we call an event.

4. It is impossible to suppose any portion of the *duration* from sunrise to the present moment not to have existed.

If you will try the experiment with yourselves, and analyze your minds, you will find that it is really impossible to think of any portion of duration as annihilated. You annihilate an hour, as you say; but there is a gap left, and it is an hour long. You annihilate an age in the flow of the eternities, and there is a gap of an age there. If you will simply notice your own thoughts, you will find that in this case, as in the case of space, we strike upon a most marvellous circumstance. The mind is so made, that it is not capable even of imagining the non-existence of time or of space. There are hundreds of proofs of this; and those who hold the materialistic philosophy do not deny the existence of this necessity in the human mind. They explain its origin and meaning in a way that I do not think clear at all; but they, with all men who understand their own mental operations, admit that all events and all objects we may annihilate in thought, but not space, not time. Moreover, we are convinced that always there was space, and always there will be; that always there was time, and always there will be.

5. It is *possible* to believe that any effect or change that has taken place might not have taken place.

6. It is *impossible* to believe that any change can have taken place without a cause.

This latter is an amazing but wholly incontrovertible fact in the mind.

Our idea of the connection of cause and effect is equally clear with our ideas concerning space and time; and the axiom which asserts that every change must have a sufficient cause is not a merely identical proposition either. I know that materialistic schools in philosophy are often saying that most axioms are simply equations between different expressions for the same thought. Whatever is, is. That, undoubtedly, is an identical proposition. It means simply, as John Stuart Mill said, that, when any proposition is true in one form of words, we have a right to affirm the same thing in any other form of words. But take an axiom which is not an identical proposition, and that is admitted even by materialists not to be one: the proposition that the equals of equals are equal to each other. (See BAIN, PROFESSOR A., *Mental and Moral Science*, English edition, p. 187.) You feel perfectly sure about that; you cannot be made to believe that that is not true. Take the proposition, that every change not only *has*, but *must* have, an adequate cause, and that is by no means an identical proposition. What is beyond the verb there does not mean only what that does which is on the first side of the verb. An identical proposition is simply an equation: what is on the left side of the verb means just what that does which is on the right of the verb. But in the proposition, that every change has and must have an adequate cause, these words on the right of the verb do not express just the meaning of the words on the left; and yet you are perfectly sure of the connection between these two phrases. Not only *has*, but *must*, you and all men put in there; and you are sure about that vast double assertion. For all time past, and all time to come, that is an axiom, you say, not only for this globe, but for the sun, and the Seven Stars, and Orion. You are sure about that truth; and, if you try ever so skilfully, you cannot make yourself believe but that every change must have an adequate cause; and yet, if you try to prove that proposition, you cannot do it by any thing that does not assume it. It is not only evident: it is self-evident. It is not evident through any other truth. It is a primitive and not a derivative truth. It is a first truth. Nevertheless, although there is no demonstration of that proposition, except by looking directly on it, or the supremest kind of demonstration,—absolute mental touch,—you are sure that it is true not only here, but everywhere; not only now, but forever. [Applause.]

7. The ideas of space and time are called in philosophy necessary ideas.

8. The belief in the connection of cause and effect is called in philosophy a necessary belief.

9. All real axioms are necessary truths.

10. All necessary truths are not only evident, but self-evident.

You may say that the proposition that it is two thousand feet from here to the gilded dome yonder is evident, but not that it is *self-evident*. You ascertain the distance by measurement and reasoning. But it is self-evident that the shortest distance between this point and that is a straight line. On that proposition you do not reason at all; and yet you are unalterably sure of it.

11. Self-evident and necessary truths are universally true; that is, everywhere and in all time.

We feel sure that it is, always was, and always will be true that a whole is greater than a part, and that the sums of equals are equals; that a thing cannot be and not be at the same time and in the same sense. We are confident that these laws hold good here, and in Orion, and everywhere.

We arrive thus at an incisive definition: —

12. *An intuition is a truth self-evident, necessary, and universal.*

It is a proposition having these three traits, — *self-evidence, necessity, and universality.*

13. Since Aristotle, these three have been the established tests of intuitive truths. (See SIR WILLIAM HAMILTON's celebrated *Note A, Appendix to* REID's *Works.*)

14. An intuition is to be distinguished from an instinct. The latter is an impulse or propensity existing independent of instruction, and prior to experience.

15. An intuition is to be distinguished from insight, emotional, reflective, or poetic.

16. An intuition is to be distinguished from inspiration or illumination, sacred or secular.

17. In scientific discussion any use of the word " intuition " to denote other than a proposition marked by self-evidence, necessity, and universality, is a violation of established usage.

18. The supreme question of philosophy is whether the self-evident, necessary, and universal truths of the mind are derived from experience, or are a part of the constitution of man brought into activity by experience, but not derived from it, nor explicable by it. Do these self-evident truths arise *à priori*, or *à*

posteriori; that is, do they exist before or only after experience?

Up to this point we are all agreed, and we have attained distinctness, I hope, as to our fundamental term. From this point onward we may not all agree; but I must venture these further propositions: —

19. This fundamental question has a new interest on account of the recent advances in philosophy, and especially in biology.

20. These advances, if the German as well as the English field is kept in view, favor the *à priori* or the intuitional school.

On one point there is no debate any longer; namely, that there are certain truths which are not only evident, but self-evident; which are absolutely necessary beliefs to the mind; and which are, therefore, universal, both in the sense of being explicitly or implicitly held by all sane men, and in that of being true in all time and in all places. (See MILL's admissions *passim*, in his *Examination of* HAMILTON's *Philosophy.*) Immanuel Kant instituted a great inquiry, you remember, as to the origin of this particular class of truths, especially of those which are not identical propositions; and now I beg leave to ask this audience whether it is not worth while for us — now that Germany has gone back to Immanuel Kant, and dares to-day build no metaphysical superstructure except on his foundations or their equivalents — to ask over again, in the light of all the recent advances of biological science, the supreme question: *Are the self evident, necessary, and universal ideas of the mind derived solely from experience, or are they a part of the original furniture of the soul, not derived at all from sensuous impressions?* [Applause.]

I am quite aware that Mr. Frothingham of New-York City, who in philosophy seems to have very little outlook beyond the North Sea, says that the Transcendentalism of which he is the historian has for the present had its day. Here is his graceful book; and, although it is only a sketch, there is large meaning between its lines in its plaintive undertone of failure. This coast of New England the Puritans made mellow soil for all seeds promising religious fruitfulness. Transcendentalism rooted itself swiftly here for that reason; but the effort was made to bring up that seed to the dignity of a tree without any sunlight from Christianity. Mr. Frothingham says the attempt has failed. I believe the seed, if it had had that light, might have lived longer. [Applause.] Let it never be forgotten that there are two classes of those who revere axiomatic truth,— the Kantian, Hamiltonian, and Coleridgian on the one side, and the purely rationalistic on the other. Mr. Frothingham says New-England Transcendentalism deliberately broke with Christianity; but in that remark he overlooks many revered names.

His own school in Transcendentalism was indeed proud to shut away from the growth of the seeds of intuitive truth the sunlight of Christianity. No oak has appeared in the twilight; but does this fact prove that the tree may not attain stately proportions if nourished by the noon? Already axiomatic truth is an oak that dreads no storms; and forests of it to-day stand in Germany, watered by the Rhine, the Elbe, and the Oder; and one day similar growths will rustle stalwart in New England, watered by the Mystic and the Charles; and the stately trees will stand on the Thames at last, in spite of its grimy mists. [Applause.] There will be for Intuitionalism in philosophy a great day, so soon as men see that the very latest philosophy knows that there is a soul external to the nervous mechanism, and that materialism must be laid aside as the result simply of lack of education. [Applause.]

21. The positions of Kant, Sir William Hamilton, and Coleridge, and not those of the rationalistic wing of Transcendentalism, are favored by the researches of the most recent German philosophy.

22. As materialism and sensationalism assert, there is in the spiritual part of man nothing which was not first in the physical sensations of the man.

23. Leibnitz long ago replied to this pretence by his famous and yet unanswered remark: There is nothing in the intellect that was not first in the sensations, *except the intellect itself.* (Nihil est in intellectu, quod non fuerit in sensu, *nisi ipse intellectus.* — LEIBNITZ, *Nouveau Essais.*)

24. It is now proved that the soul is a force external to the nervous mechanism, and that the molecular motions of the particles of the latter are a closed circuit not transmutable into the activities of the former.

25. *We know now, therefore, that, besides what furniture sensation and association give to the soul, there are in us, wholly independent of experience, the soul and the plan of the soul.* [Applause.]

26. Of this plan, which must be the basis of all philosophy relating to man, the self-evident, necessary, and universal truths, or the intuitions on the one hand, and the organic or constitutional instincts on the other, are a revelation.

27. *Every organic instinct must be assumed to have its correlate to match it.*

28. *Every really intuitive belief must be held to be correct.* [Applause.]

Proof that there is a soul is proof that there is a plan of the soul.

It is now a commonplace of science that the universality of law is incontrovertible. If the soul has an existence, it has a plan, for the universality of law requires that every thing that exists should have a plan; and, if the soul exists, there is no doubt a plan according to which it was made, and according to which it should act.

When, therefore, we prove that the soul is something different from matter, or that it is as external to the nervous system as light to the eye, and the pulsations of the air to the ear; when physiological science, led by the Lotzes and Ulricis and Beales, asserts that the soul is possibly the occupant of a spiritual body; or when, not going as far as that, we simply say there is a soul, — we affirm by implication that it is made upon a plan. In the light of the best biological science of our day, it is incontrovertible that we have in man two things at least that did not originate in his senses; namely, the soul and the plan of the soul. [Applause.] That is not a proposition of small importance. It means that these necessary beliefs, these self-evident truths, these first principles, inhere in the very plan of our soul; and that they are, therefore, a supreme revelation to us from the Author of that plan.

Self-evident truths thus take hold of the roots of the world. If, now, I raise the question whether instinctive beliefs, whether the first truths, which Aristotle said no man could desert and find surer, whether self-evident propositions, are not made self-evident of necessity by the very structure of our souls, you will not think I am running into mysticism, will you? You believe there is a soul, and you hold that every thing is made on a plan; or that from the eyelash that looks on Orion, up to Orion itself, there is no escape from the universality of law: therefore, you must hold, that, since every thing is made on a plan, the soul itself is. Just as you know that your hand was not made to shut toward the back, but toward the front, you know that the soul is made according to a certain plan. If we can find out that plan, we can ascertain what is the best way in which to live. It is said we can know nothing; but do we not already know that there is a best way to live, and that it is best to live the best way, as assuredly as we know that our hand was not made to shut toward the back, but toward the front? I think I know that [applause] in spite of all the wooden songs of materialism.

Germany yet listens to Immanuel Kant, and to those who, succeeding him with the microscope and scalpel, have carried biological knowledge far beyond its state in his time, and are now asserting not only the existence of the soul, and its independence of the body, but that, because law is universal, the soul must be made on a plan; and that, therefore, the supreme question of moral science and intellectual philosophy, and of all research that founds itself on mere organism, must be to ascertain what the plan of the soul is, in order that, through a knowledge of the plan, we may learn to conform to it. [Applause.]

What, then, must philosophy to-day call the supreme tests of truth?

In the ceiling of this temple will you imagine a great circle to be drawn, and will you call one quarter of it Intuition, another quarter Instinct, another Experiment, another Syllogism? Let our attempts at arriving at certitude all consist of endeavors to rise to the centre from which all these arcs are drawn. If you will show me what the intuitions are, and do that clearly, I can almost admit that you may strike the whole circle from simply a knowledge of that quadrant. I know, that, if you can inductively determine any curve of the circle, you can then determine deductively the whole. But, my friends, we have seen too many failures in this high attempt to describe the circle of the universe by determining three points only. No doubt through any three points a circle may be drawn; but so vast is the circle of infinities and eternities, that our poor human compasses cannot be trusted, if we use one of these quadrants only. *Let us be intuitionalists, but much else.* Let us test quadrant by quadrant around the whole circle of research. Let us conjoin the testimony of Intuition, Instinct, Experiment, and Syllogism. Show me accord between your quadrant of Intuition and your quadrant of Instinct, and between these two and the quadrant of Experiment, — this latter is the English quarter of the heavens, and that of Intuition is the German, — and between these three and the quadrant of Syllogism; and, with these four supreme tests of truth agreeing, I know enough for the cancelling of the orphanage of Doubt. I know not every thing; but I assuredly can find a way through all multiplex labyrinths between God and man, and will with confidence ascend through the focus of the four quadrants into God's bosom. [Applause.]

Archbishop Whately said, that, the wider the circle of illumination, the greater the circle of surrounding darkness. Acknowledging that this is true, we shall be devoutly humble face to face with inexplicable portions of the universe. Nevertheless, let us, with the faith of Emerson, with the insight of Theodore Parker, with the acuteness of John Stuart Mill, as well as with the deadly precision of Kant, and of all clear and devout souls since the world began, hold unalterably, in this age of unrest and orphanage, that, if these four quadrants agree, we may implicitly trust them as tests of truth. [Applause.] The supreme rules of certitude were never more visible than in our distracted day; and they are Intuition, Instinct, Experiment, Syllogism. Each is a subtle verification of every other. Let us image these vast quadrants of research as so many gigantic reflectors of a light not their own. At the focal point of the four, Religious Science, strictly so called, lights its immortal torch. [Applause.]

II.

TRANSCENDENTALISM IN NEW ENGLAND.

THE SIXTIETH LECTURE IN THE BOSTON MONDAY LECTURE-
SHIP, DELIVERED IN TREMONT TEMPLE JAN. 8.

"Φήμη δ'οὔποτε πάμπαν ἀπόλλυται ἥν τινα πολλοὶ
Λαοὶ φημίζουσι· θεός νύ τις ἐστὶ καὶ αὐτή."
HESIOD: *Works and Days.*

"LET us do what we can to rekindle the smouldering, nigh quenched fire on the altar. The remedy is first soul, and second soul, and evermore soul."—EMERSON: *Address at Cambridge,* July 15, 1838.

II.

TRANSCENDENTALISM IN NEW ENG- LAND.

PRELUDE ON CURRENT EVENTS.

A SERIOUS man must rejoice to have Christianity tested philosophically, historically, and in every great way, but not in a certain small, light, and inwardly coarse way, of which the world has had enough, and is tired. Yesterday the most scholarly representative of what calls itself Free Religion told Boston that the Author of Christianity is historically only an idolized memory inwreathed with mythical fictions. Will you allow me to say that the leading universities of Germany, through their greatest specialists in exegetical and historical research, have decisively given up that opinion? Thirty or forty years ago it was proclaimed there in rationalistic lecture-rooms very emphatically: to-day such lecture-rooms are empty, and those of the opposing schools are crowded. On the stately grounds of Sans Souci, where Frederick the Great and Voltaire had called out to the culture of Europe, "*Ecrasez l'infame!*" King William and his queen lately entertained an

Evangelical Alliance gathered from the Indus, the Nile, the Danube, the Rhine, the Thames, and the Mississippi. Histories of the rise and progress and decline of German Rationalism, and especially of the power of the Mythical Theory, have been appearing abundantly for the last fifteen years in the most learned portions of the literature of Germany. The incontrovertible fact is, that every prominent German university, except Heidelberg, is now under predominant evangelical influences. Heidelberg is nearly empty of theological students. Lord Bacon said that the best materials for prophecy are the unforced opinions of young men. Against twenty-four theological students at rationalistic Heidelberg there were lately at evangelical Halle two hundred and eighty-two; at evangelical Berlin two hundred and eighty; and at hyper-evangelical Leipzig four hundred and twelve.

Before certain recent discussions and discoveries on the field of research into the history of the origin of Christianity, the rationalistic lecture-rooms were crowded, and the evangelical empty. It is notorious that such teachers as Tholuck, Julius Müller, Dorner, Twesten, Ullmann, Lange, Rothe, and Tischendorf, most of whom began their professorships at their universities with great unpopularity, on account of their opposition to rationalistic views, are now particularly honored on that very account. (See article on the "Decline of Rationalism in the German Universities," *Bibliotheca Sacra*, October, 1875.)

We often have offered to us in Boston the crumbs

from German philosophical tables; and, although I must not speak harshly, the truth must be told, namely, that the faithful in the uneducated ranks of scepticism — I do not deny that there are vast masses of Orthodoxy uneducated also — are not infrequently fed on cold remnants swept away with derision from the scholarly repasts of the world. If you will open the biography of David Friedrich Strauss, by Zeller, his admiring friend, and a professor at Heidelberg, you will read these unqualified words: "Average theological liberalism pressed forward eagerly to renounce all compromising association with Strauss after he published the last statement of his mythical theory." (See ZELLER, PROFESSOR EDUARD, "*Strauss in his Life and Writings*," English translation, London, 1874, pp. 135, 141, 143.) It did so under irresistible logical pressure, and especially because recent discoveries have carried back the dates of the New-Testament literature fifty years.

Thirty years ago it used to be thought that the earliest date at which the New-Testament literature can be shown to have been received as of equal authority with the Old was about A.D. 130; but, as all scholars will tell you, even Baur admitted that Paul's chief Epistles were genuine, and were written before the year 60. This admission is fatal to the mythical theory put forth by Strauss when he was a young man, and now for twenty years marked as juvenile by the best scholarship of Germany. These letters of Paul, written at that date, are incontrovertible proof that the leading traits of the character of the Author of Christianity, as given in the so-called mythical Gospels, were familiar to the Christian world within twenty-five years after his death (THAYER, PROFESSOR J. HENRY, of Andover, *Boston Lectures*, 1871, p. 372). There is now in the hands of scholars incontrovertible evidence that even the Gospels had acquired authority with the earliest churches as early as A.D. 125. Schenkel, Renan, Keim, Weizsäcker, and others widely removed from the traditional views, teach that the Fourth Gospel itself could not have appeared later than a few years after the beginning of the second century. (See FISHER, PROFESSOR GEORGE P., *Essays on the Supernatural Origin of Christianity*, 1870, *Preface*, p. xxxviii.) These discoveries explain the new attitude of German scholarship. They carry back the indubitable traces of the New-Testament literature more than fifty years. They shut the colossal shears of chronology upon the theories of Baur, Strauss, and Renan. They narrow by so much the previously too narrow room used by these theories to explain the growth of myths and legends. Strauss demands a century after the death of Paul for his imaginative additions to Christianity to grow up in. It is now established that not only not a century, but not a quarter of a century, can be had for this purpose. The upper date of A.D. 34, and the lower date of A.D. 60, as established by exact research, are the two merciless blades of the shears between which the latest and most deftly-woven web of doubt is cut in two. [Applause.] There is no room for that course of mythical development which the Tübingen school describes. As a sect in biblical criticism, this school has perished. Its history has been written in more than one tongue (THAYER, PROFESSOR J. HENRY, *Criticism Confirmatory of the Gospels, Boston Lectures*, 1871, pp. 363, 364, 371).

Chevalier Bunsen once wrote to Thomas Arnold this incisive exclamation : " The idea of men writing mythic histories between the time of Livy and Tacitus, and Saint Paul mistaking such for realities ! " ARNOLD's *Life, Letter* cxliv.) Paul had opportunity to know the truth, and was, besides, one of the boldest and acutest spirits of his own or of any age. *Was Paul a dupe?* [Applause.]

But who does not know the history of the defeat of sceptical school after sceptical school on the rationalistic side of the field of exegetical research? The naturalistic theory was swallowed by the mythical theory, and the mythical by the tendency theory, and the tendency by the legendary theory, and each of the four by time. [Applause.] Strauss laughs at Paulus, Baur at Strauss, Renan at Baur, the hourglass at all. [Applause.] " Under his guidance," says Strauss of Paulus (*New Life of Jesus*, English translation, p. 18), "we tumble into the mire; and assuredly dross, not gold, is the issue to which his method of interpretation generally leads." " Up to the present day," says Baur of Strauss (*Krit. Unters. über die canonische Evangel.*, 121, 40 – 71), "the mythical theory has been rejected by every man of education." And yet New-York lips teach it here in modern Athens! [Applause.] "Insufficient," says Renan of Baur (*Étude d'Hist. Rel.*, 163), "is what he leaves existing of the Gospels to account for the faith of the apostles." He makes the Pauline and Petrine factions account for the religion, and the religion account for the Pauline and Petrine factions. "Criticism has run all to leaves," said Strauss (see ZELLER, *Life of Strauss*, p. 143) in his bitter disappointment at the failure of his final volume.

Appropriately was there carried on Richter's coffin to his grave a manuscript of his last work, — a discussion in proof of the immortality of the soul: appropriately might there have been carried on Strauss's coffin to his grave his last work, restating his mythical theory, if only that theory had not, as every scholar knows, died and been buried before its author. [Applause.]

The supreme question concerning the origin of the New-Testament literature is now, whether, in less than thirty years intervening between the death of the Author of Christianity and A.D. 60, in which Paul's Epistles are known to have become authorities, there is room enough in the age of Livy and Tacitus for the growth and inwreathing of mythical fictions around an idolized memory lying in the dim haze of the past. An unscholarly and discredited theory was presented to you yesterday gracefully, but not forcefully.

Let us see what a vigorous and unpartisan mind says on the same topic. "I know men," said Napoleon at St. Helena — the record is authentic; read it in Liddons' Bampton Lectures on the Divinity of Our Lord, the best recent book on that theme, — "I know men, and I tell you that Jesus of Nazareth was not a man." Daniel Webster, on his dying-bed, wrote on the marble of his tombstone "The Sermon on the Mount cannot be a merely human production." Renan was particularly cited to you yesterday; but when I went into the study of Professor Dorner, Schleiermacher's successor, at Berlin, and conversed with him about the greatest sceptics of Europe, I came to the name of Renan, and said, "What are we to think of his 'Life of Jesus'?"

"Das ist Nichts," he answered, and added no more. "That is nothing." [Applause.]

No doubt, in the fume and foam and froth of literary brilliancy serving a lost, bad cause, there may be iridescence, as well as in the enduring opal and pearl; but, while the colors seven flashed from the fragile spray are as beautiful as foam and froth, they are also just as substantial. [Applause.]

THE LECTURE.

Side by side under the lindens in the great cemetery of Berlin lie Fitche and Hegel; and I am transcendentalist enough myself to have walked one lonely day, four miles, from the tombs of Neander and Schleiermacher, on the hill south of the city, to the quiet spot where the great philosophers of transcendentalism lie at rest till the heavens be no more. I treasure among the mementos of travel some broad myrtle-leaves which I plucked from the sods that lie above these giants in philosophy; and, if I to-day cast a little ridicule upon the use some of their disciples have made of the great tenets of the masters, you will not suppose me to be irreverent towards any fountain-head of intuitive, axiomatic, self-evident truth. You wish, and I, too, wish, cool draughts out of the Castalian spring of axioms. You are, and I, too, am, thirsty for certainty; and I find it only in the sure four tests of truth,—intuition, instinct, experiment, syllogism,—all agreeing. [Applause.] But of the four tests, of course the first is chief, head and shoulders above all the rest.

Even in Germany the successors of the great transcendentalists have made sport for the ages; and no doubt here in New England it was to have been expected that there should be some sowing of "transcendental wild-oats." [Applause.] That phrase is the incisive language of a daughter of transcendentalism honored by this generation, and likely to be honored by many more. I am asking you to look to-day at the erratic side of a great movement, the right wing and centre of which I respect, but the left wing of which, or that which broke with Christianity, has brought upon itself self-confessed defeat.

What has been the outcome of breaking with Christianity in the name of intuitive truth in Germany? Take up the latest advices, which it is my duty, as an outlook committee for this audience, to keep before you, and you will find that Immanuel Hermann Fichte, the son of this man at whose grave

I stood in Berlin, has just passed into the Unseen Holy; and that, as his last legacy, he left to the ages a work entitled "Questions and Considerations concerning the Newest Form of German Speculation." When, one day, the great Fichte heard the drums of Napoleon beat in the streets of Berlin, he closed a lecture by announcing that the next would be given when Prussia had become free; and then enlisted against the conqueror, and kept his word. The son has had a more quiet life than the father; but he has given himself exclusively to philosophy. The second Fichte was the founder of the "Journal of Speculative Philosophy," now conducted by Ulrici and Wirth; and he has lived through much. He knew his father's system presumably well. Has it led to pantheism or materialism with him, as it has with some others? *If Emerson has made pantheism a logical outcome of Fichte's teachings, what has Fichte's son made of them?* The son of the great Fichte has been a professor at Dusseldorf and Bonn, and, since 1842, at Tübingen. He is a specialist in German philosophy if ever there was one; and his latest production was a history of his own philosophical school. He attempted to show that the line of sound philosophy in Germany is represented by three great names,—Leibnitz and Kant and Lotze. You do not care to have from me an outline of his work; and perhaps, therefore, you will allow me to read the summary of it given by your North-American Review, for that certainly ought to be free from partisanship. Thus Fichte loftily writes to Zeller, the biographer of Strauss, and his positions are a sign of the times: —

"Ethical theism is now master of the situation. The attempt to lose sight of the personal God in nature, or to subordinate his transcendence over the universe to any power immanent in the universe, and especially the tendency to deny the theology of ethics, and to insist only upon the reign of force, are utterly absurd, and are meeting their just condemnation." [Applause.] (*North-American Review*, January, 1877, p. 147.)

Concord once listened to Germany. Will it continue to listen? Cambridge cannot show at the foot of her text-book pages five English names where she can show ten German. In the footnotes of learned works you will find German authorities a dozen times where you can find English six, or American three. Let us appeal to no temporary swirl of currents, but to a Gulf Stream. Of course, history is apt to be misleading, unless we take it in long ranges. Read Sir William Hamilton's celebrated summary (*Note A, Appendix to* REID'S *works*), if you wish to see the whole gulf current of belief in self-evident truth since Aristotle. But here in Germany is a vast stretch of modern philosophical discussion, beginning with Leibnitz, running on through Kant, and so coming down to Lotze; and it is all on the line of intuitive truth, and it never has broken with Christianity, nor been drawn into either the Charybdis of materialism or the Scylla of pantheism. [Applause.]

The latest and acutest historian of German theology, Schwartz of Gotha, says that Strauss designates not so much a beginning as an end, and that the supreme lack in his system is twofold, — the absence of historical insight and of religious sensibility. Now, I will not deny that rationalism in New England, with eight generations of Puritan culture behind it, has often shown religious sensitiveness. Some transcendentalists who have broken with Christianity I reverence so far forth as they retain here in New England a degree of religious sensibility which is often utterly unknown among rationalists abroad. Heaven cause my tongue to cleave to the roof of my mouth if ever I say aught ironical, or in any way derogatory, of that consciousness of God which underlay the vigor of Theodore Parker, which is the transfiguring thing in Emerson, and which, very much further down in the list of those who are shy of Christianity, is yet the glory of their thinking, and of their reverence for art, and is especially the strength of their philanthropic endeavors! [Applause.] We have no France for a neighbor; wars have not stormed over America as they have over Europe; and it cannot yet be said, even of our erratics, as undoubtedly it can be of many French and German ones, that they have lost the consciousness of God.

What is Transcendentalism?

You will not suspect me of possessing the mood of that acute teacher, who, on the deck of a Mississippi steamer, was asked this question, and replied,

"See the holes made in the bank yonder by the swallows. Take away the bank, and leave the apertures, and this is Transcendentalism." The answer to this is the certainty that we are all bank-swallows. The right wing and the centre of this social, twittering human race live in these apertures, as well as the left wing; and it would be of little avail to ridicule the self-evident truths on which our own peace depends. I affirm simply that Transcendentalism of the left wing has not been consistent with Transcendentalism itself.

My general proposition is, that rationalistic Transcendentalism in New England is not Transcendentalism, but, at the last analysis, Individualism.

Scholars will find that on this occasion, as on many others, discussion here is purposely very elementary.

1. The plan of the physical organism is not in the food by which the organism is sustained.

2. The mechanism by which the assimilation of food is effected exists before the food is received.

3. But, until the food is received, that mechanism does not come into operation.

4. The plan of the spiritual organism is not in the impressions received through sensation and association.

5. The fundamental laws of thought exist in the plan of the soul anterior to all sensation or association.

6. But they are brought into operation only by experience through sensation and association.

7. It is absurd to say that the plan of the body is produced by its food.

8. It is equally absurd to say that the plan, or fundamental intuitive beliefs of the soul, are produced by sensation and association.

9. Therefore, as the plan of the body does not have its origin in the food of the body, so the plan of the mind does not have its origin in the food of the mind.

You receive food, and a certain plan in your physical organism distributes it after it is received, assimilates it, and you are entirely sure that the mechanism involved in this process exists before the food. It may be that every part of my physical system is made up of food and drink which I have taken, or of air which I have breathed; and yet there is one thing in me that the food did not give me, or the air; and that is the plan of my physical organism. [Applause.] Not in the gases, not in the fluids, not in the solids, was there the plan of these lenses in the eye, or of this harp of three thousand strings in the ear.

Besides all the materials which go to make up a watch, you must have the plan of the watch. If I were to place a book on my right here, and then take another copy of the book and tear it into shreds, and cast these down on the left, it would not be lawful to say that I have on one side the same that I have on the other. In one case the volume is arranged in an intelligible order: in the other it is chaotic. Besides the letters, we must have the coordination of the letters in the finished volume. So in man's organism it is perfectly evident that the food which we eat, and which does, indeed, build every thing in us, is not us; for the plan of us is something existing before that food enters the system, and that plan separates the different elements, and distributes them in such a way as to bring out the peculiarities of each individual organism.

Now, whether or not you admit that there is a spiritual organism behind the physical, whether or not you agree with your Beales and Lotzes and Ulricis in asserting that the scientific method requires that we should suppose that there is in us a spiritual organism which weaves the physical, you will at least admit, that, so far as the individual experience is concerned, we have within us laws, fundamental, organic, and, if not innate, at least connate. They came into the world with us; they are a part of the plan on which we are made. When we touch the external world with the outer senses, and the inner world with the inner senses, no doubt food is coming to our souls; but that plan is the law according to which all our experiences through sensation and association are distributed.

10. The school of sensationalism in philosophy maintains that the soul's laws are only an accumulation of inheritances.

11. To that school, self-evident truths themselves are simply those which result from an unvarying and the largest experience; or those which have been deeply engraved on our physical organisms by the

uniform sensations of our whole line of ancestors back to the earliest and simplest form of life.

12. Human experience cannot embrace all space and time.

13. Sensationalism in philosophy, therefore, which holds that all the intuitive or axiomatic truths arise from experience, must deny that we can be sure that these truths are true in all space and time.

14. But we are thus sure; and sensationalism is wrecked on its palpable inability to explain by experience this confessed certainty.

Face to face with this inadequate explanation which evolution offers for the self-evident, necessary, and universal truths of the soul, let us look at the worst.

It matters to me very little how my eyes came into existence, if only they see accurately. You say conscience was once only a bit of sensitive matter in a speck of jelly. You affirm, that, by the law of the survival of the fittest, in the struggle of many jelly-specks with each other for existence, one peculiarly-vigorous jelly-speck obtained the advantage of its brethren, and so became the progenitor of many vigorous jelly-specks. Then these vigorous jelly-specks made new war on each other; and individuals, according to the law of heredity with variation, having now and then fortunate endowments, survived, and transmitted these, to become better and better, until the jelly-specks produce the earliest seaweed. By and by a mollusk appears under the law of the survival of the fittest, and then higher and higher forms, till at last, through infinite chance and mischance, man is produced. Somewhere and somehow the jelly-specks get not only an intellect, not only artistic perception, but conscience and will, and this far-reaching longing for immortality, this sense that there is a Mind superior to ours on which we are dependent. Now, for a moment, admit that this theory of evolution, which Professor Dawson, in an article in the last number of the "International Review," on Huxley in New York, says will be regarded by the next age as one of the most mysterious of illusions, is true, the supreme question yet remains, — whether my conscience is authority.

Take something merely physical, like the eyes. When I was a jelly-speck of the more infirm sort, or at least when I was a fish, I saw something, and what I saw I saw. When I was a lichen, although I was not a sensitive-plant, I felt something, and what I felt I felt. So when, at last, these miraculous lenses began to appear, as the law of the survival of the fittest rough-hewed them age after age, I saw better and better; but what I saw I saw: and to-day I feel very sure that the deliverance of the eyes is accurate. I am not denying here any of the facts as to our gradual acquisition of the knowledge of distance and of dimension; that comes from the operation of all the senses; but we feel certain that what we see we see.

Suppose, then, that, in this grand ascent from the jelly-speck to the archangel, the process of evolution shall at last make our eyes as powerful as the best telescopes of the present day. It will yet plainly be true, will it not, that what we see we see? and as the eyes are now good within their range, so, when they become telescopic, they will be good within their range. Just so, even if we hold to the evolutionary hypothesis in its extremest claims, we must hold, that, if conscience was good for any thing when it was rudimentary, it is good now in its higher stage of development. If by and by it shall become telescopic, what it sees it will see. [Applause.] I will not give up for an instant the authority of *connate*, although you deny all *innate* truth. You may show me that fatalism is the result of your evolutionary hypothesis; you may prove to me that immortality cannot be maintained if your philosophy is true; you may, indeed, assert, as Häckel does, "that there is no God but necessity," if you are an evolutionist of the thorough-going type, that is, not only a Darwinian, but an Häckelian. But let Häckel's consistent atheistic evolutionism, which Germany rejects with scorn, be adopted, and it will yet remain true that there is a plan in man; and that, while there is a plan in man, there will be a best way to live; and that, while there is a best way to live, it will be best to live the best way. [Applause.]

There is, however, no sign of the progress of the Häckelian theory of evolution toward general acceptance. On every side you are told that evolution is more and more the philosophy of science. But which form of the theory of evolution is meant? The Darwinian is *a* theory, the Häckelian is *the* theory, of evolution.

15. Observing our mental operations, we very easily convince ourselves that we are sure of the truth of some propositions, concerning which neither we nor the race have had experience.

16. If it be true that all these certainties that we call self-evident arise simply from experience, it must be shown that our certainties do not reach beyond our experience.

It is very sure, is it not, that the sun might rise to-morrow morning in the west? Neither we nor our ancestors have had any experience of its rising there. Space is a necessary idea, but the rising of the sun in the east is not; and yet our experience of the one is as invariable as that of the other. That blazing mass of suns we call Orion might have its stellar points differently arranged; and yet I never saw Orion in any shape other than that which it now possesses. I am perfectly confident that the gems on the sword-hilt of Orion might be taken away, or never have been in existence; but I never yet saw Orion without seeing there the flashing of the jewels on the hilt of his sword.

John Stuart Mill would say, and so would George Henry Lewes, — whose greatest distinction, by the way, is, that he is the husband of Marian Evans, the authoress of "Daniel Deronda," — that, although my own experience never has shown to me Orion in any other shape than that which it now possesses, perhaps my ability to give it another shape in thought may arise from some experience in the race behind me. We are told by the school of evolution, that it is not our individual experience that explains our necessary ideas, but the transmitted experience of the race behind us. We have inherited nervous changes, from the whole range of the development of the species; and so, somewhere and somehow in the past, there must have been an experience which gives you the capacity to say that the sun may rise in the west, and that Orion might have another shape. But is it not tolerably sure that none of my grandfathers or great-grandfathers, back to the jelly-speck, ever saw the sun rise in.the west? The human race never saw Orion in any other shape. The truth is, that experience goes altogether too short a distance to account for the wide range of such a certainty, as that every effect, not only here, but everywhere, must have a cause.

17. Experience does not teach what *must* be, but only what *is;* but we know that every change not only *has*, but *must* have, a cause.

I never had any experience in the Sun, or in the Seven Stars. I never paced about the Pole with Ursa Major, across the breadth of one of whose eyelashes my imagination cannot pass without fainting; I know nothing of the thoughts of Saggitarius, as he bends his bow of fire yonder in the southern heavens: but this I do know, that everywhere and in all time every change *must* have a cause. You are certain of the universality of every necessary truth. How are you to account for that certainty by any known experience?

18. *We cannot explain by experience a certainty that goes beyond experience.*

John Stuart Mill, perfectly honest and perfectly luminous, comes squarely up to this difficulty, and says in so many words, "There may be worlds in which two and two do not make four, and where a change need not have a cause." (*Examination of* Hamilton's *Philosophy;* see, also, Mill's *Logic*, book iii. chap. xxi.) So clearly does he see this objection, that, astounding some of his adherents, he made this very celebrated admission, which has done more to cripple the philosophy of sensationalism, probably, than any other event in its history for the last twenty-five years. Even mathematical axioms may be false. You and I, gentlemen, feel, and must feel, that this conclusion is arbitrary; that it is not true to the constitution of man; that we have within us something which asserts not only the present earthly certainty, that every change must have a cause, but that forever and forever, in all time to come, and backward through all time past, this law holds.

19. Everywhere, all exact science assumes the universal applicability of all true axioms in all time and in all places.

Rejecting in the name of exact science, therefore, Mill's startling paradox, we must conclude that we are not loyal to the indications of our own constitution, unless we say that there is in us a possibility of reaching certainty beyond experience. Now to do that is to reach a transcendental truth.

20. Transcendental truths are simply those necessary, self-evident, axiomatic truths which transcend

experience. Transcendentalism is the science of such self-evident, axiomatic, necessary truths.

Kant gave this name to a part of his philosophy, and it is by no means a word of reproach. Of course I am treating Transcendentalism, not with an eye on New England merely, but with due outlook on this form of philosophy throughout the world, especially upon Coleridge and Wordsworth, Mansel and Maurice, and Sir William Hamilton, and Leibnitz and Kant and Lotze. I am not taking Transcendentalism in that narrow meaning in which some opponents of it may have represented it to themselves. That every change, here and everywhere, not only has, but must have, a cause, is a transcendental truth: it transcends experience. So the certainty that here and everywhere things which are equal to the same thing are equal to each other is a transcendental certainty. Our conviction in the moral field that sin can be a quality only of voluntary action is a transcendental fact. This moral axiom we feel is sure in all time and in all space. There are moral intuitions as well as intellectual. There are æsthetic intuitions, I believe; and they will yet produce a science of the beautiful, as those of the intellect and the conscience produce sciences of the true and the good. If man have no freedom of will, he cannot commit sins in the strict sense, for demerit implies free agency; and we feel that this is a moral certainty, and you cannot go behind it.

Coleridge complained much in his time of "that compendious philosophy which contrives a theory for spirit by nicknaming matter, and in a few hours can qualify its dullest disciples to explain the *omne scibile* by reducing all things to impressions, ideas, and sensations " (*Biograph. Literaria*, chap. xii.). What would he have said to the recent attempt by Tyndall to nickname matter, and call it mind, or a substance with a spiritual and physical side? Only the other day, Lewes endeavored to nickname sensation, and call it both the internal law of the soul and the external sense. Will you please listen to an amazing definition out of the latest, and perhaps the subtlest attempt to justify sensationalism in philosophy? " The sensational hypothesis is acceptable, if by sense we understand *sensibility and its laws of operation*. This obliterates the very distinction insisted on by the other school. It includes all psychical phenomena under the rubric of sensibility. It enables pyschological analysis to be consistent and exhaustive." (LEWES's *Problems of Life and Mind*, 1874, vol. i. p. 208.)

This passage affirms, that, if you will say food is the body, food will explain the body. If you will take the metal which goes to make the watch as not only the metal, but the plan of the watch too, then your matter and your plan put together will be the watch. He wants sensation to mean sensibility and its laws; that is to say, he would have the very fundamental principles of our soul included in this term, which, thus interpreted, I should say, with Coleridge, is a nickname. Such a definition concedes much by implication; but Lewes concedes in so many words, that,

" if by sense is meant simply the five senses, the reduction of all knowledge to a sensuous origin is absurd."

Such is the latest voice, my friends, from the opponents of the Intuitional school in philosophy; and it is substantially a confession, that, unless a new definition be given to sensation, the sensational philosophy must be given up. Stuart Mill affirmed that two and two might make seven in Orion, and that a change possibly might not have a cause in the North Star. He was forced to no greater straits than the husband of George Eliot is, when he says that the only escape from the necessity of adopting the intuitional philosophy is to assume its definitions as those of the sensational school itself. Bloody, unjust exploits, are often performed by lawless men on the battle-field of philosophy; but, after all, the ages like to see fair play. We must observe the rules of the game. When Greek wrestlers stood up together, the audience and the judges saw to it that the rules of the game were observed. These were defined rigidly. All religious science asks of scepticism, in this age or any other, is, that it will observe the laws of the scientific method. We must adhere to the rules of the game; and when established definitions are nicknamed, as they now are by materialism, suicide is confession. [Applause.]

III.

THEODORE PARKER'S ABSOLUTE RELIGION.

THE SIXTY-FIRST LECTURE IN THE BOSTON MONDAY LECTURESHIP, DELIVERED IN TREMONT TEMPLE JAN. 15.

"Si l'expérience interne immédiate pouvait nous tromper, il ne saurait y avoir pour moi aucune vérité de fait, j'ajoute ni de raison." — LEIBNITZ.

> "Corpus enim per se communis deliquat esse,
> Sensus; quo nisi prima fides fundata valebit,
> Haud erit, occultis de rebus quo referentes,
> Confirmare animi, quicquam ratione queamus."
> LUCRETIUS.

III.

THEODORE PARKER'S ABSOLUTE RELIGION.

PRELUDE ON CURRENT EVENTS.

It was once my fortune in the city of Edinburgh to visit the famous room in which Burke and Hare committed fourteen murders by dropping men through a trap-door, and afterwards strangling them, that they might obtain human skins to sell to physicians for medical purposes. Across the street from this classical cellar of horrors, there used to be an old tan-loft, in the midst of a population one quarter of which was on the poor-roll, and another quarter measly with the unreportable vices. When Thomas Chalmers was a professor in the University of Edinburgh, he deliberately selected this verminous and murderous quarter as the spot in which to begin a crucial trial of a plan of his for the solution of the problem as to the management of the poor in great cities. It was his audacious belief, that there is no population so degraded in any of our large towns, that it will not maintain Christian institutions if once these are fairly set on foot. Southward from the gray cliff on which Edinburgh's renowned historic castle stands, he took the district called the West Port, with a population of about two thousand, and divided it into twenty sub-districts, and appointed over each one a visitor, sometimes a lady, and sometimes a gentleman. It was the business of these angels of mercy to go once each week into every family, without exception, and to leave there, not often money, not always food, but an invitation to the children to attend the industrial and religious schools, and to parents to become members of the church of which Chalmers had the supreme courage to begin the formation in the old tan-loft, face to face with that room in which fourteen murders had been committed. This visitation was made thorough. Every person aided was taught to pay something, however little, for the support of the school and church opened for his benefit. A feeling of self-respect was thus systematically cultivated. This was an essential portion of the Chalmerian plan. The enterprise of founding a self-supporting church among the poor and vile in the West Port of Edinburg was in five years so successful, that, out of a hundred and thirty-two communicants, more than a hundred in the church were from the population of the West Port. Not a child of suitable age lived in the district and was not in school. A savings bank had been instituted, a washing-house had been opened, an industrial school had been maintained day and night in the secular portions of the week. Better than all, the entire expense of all these institutions, amounting to thirty thousand dollars a year, was paid by the West Port; and that improved section of paupers had money enough every year to contribute seventy pounds for benevolent purposes outside the borders of their own territory. [Applause.]

It was thought this enterprise would fail on Chalmers's death; but, so far from doing so, his famous territorial church is to-day in a flourishing condition, and has been extensively copied in Scotland. His plan of territorial visitation and self-supporting religious enterprises has become one of the best hopes of the poor in Scotland's great cities. I worshipped once in the West Port church, and found there the names of fifty or sixty church-officers of various kinds posted up on the doors, and arranged in couples, with their specific districts for visitation definitely named on the bulletin. A hushed, crowded audience of the cleanly and respectable poor listened to a vigorous address, and made touching contributions for religious purposes. Mr. Tasker, the pastor whom Chalmers had chosen, said to me at his tea-table, "There is nae rat in yon kirk. I told the people at the first I would na minister to a congregation of paupers. Every steady attendant pays more or less, and so keeps up self-respect. He helps the poor most who helps them to help themselves. Yon kirk is self-supporting."

Chalmers did not live to see these larger results; but he saw enough to cause him to anticipate them; and he perfectly understood the vast political importance of the complex problem he had attacked. He foresaw that more and more the population of the world must mass itself in cities. His experiment he did not consider complete without aid from the civil arm, which ought to second the efforts of philanthropy by executing all righteous public law.

Most eloquently Chalmers wrote in his advancing years: "I would again implore the aid of the authorities for the removal of all these moral, and the aid of the Sanitary Board for the removal of all those physical, nuisances and discomforts which are found to exist within a territory so full of misery and vice at present, yet so full of promise for the future. *Could I gain this help from our men in power, and this co-operation from the Board of Health, then with the virtue which lies in education, and, above all, the hallowing influence of the gospel of Jesus Christ, I should look, though in humble dependence on the indispensable grace from on high, for such a result as, at least in its first beginnings, I could interpret into the streaks and dawnings of a better day; when, after the struggles and discomforts of thirty years, I might depart in peace, and leave the further prosecution of our enterprise with comfort and calmness in the hands of another generation.*" (See Memoirs of Chalmers, by REVEREND WILLIAM HANNA, London, 1859, chapter entitled "The West Port," p. 413.)

Chalmers's celebrated scheme for throttling the troubles of the poor and vicious in great towns embraced these three provisions: —

Territorial visitation, or systematic going about from house to house doing good.

Self-supporting benevolent and religious institutions among the needy and degraded.

The execution of righteous law against the tempters and fleecers of the poor. [Applause.]

Gentlemen, some of us here are young yet; and we have heard the departing footsteps of the great problem of slavery in our own land. We who have in expectation our brief careers are listening to the first heavy footfalls of a far more menacing problem, that concerning greed and fraud in politics, when the gigantic and crescent party-spoils of a land greater than Cæsar ever ruled are made the reward of merely party success. But behind that black angel, with his far-spreading Gehenna wings shadowing both our ocean shores, some of us who are looking forward, and are rash, as you think, can but notice the stealthy advance of another fell spirit with whom we must contend; and his name is, The Metropolitan. He is the genius that presides over the neglect of the poor in great towns. He is the archfiend, who, as the growth of all means of intercommunication, causes the world to mass its population more and more in cities, breathes upon many fashionable churches the sirocco of luxury, and leaves them swinging in hammocks, attached, on the one side, to the Cross, and on the other to the forefinger of Mammon, and not easy even then, unless they are eloquently fanned [applause], and sprinkled, as the Eastern host sprinkles his guest, with lavender ease. [Applause.] Meanwhile, the fiend Metropolitan Evil advances with a footfall that already sometimes rocks the continent, and yet it appears to be unheard. Now and then the cloven, ominous hoof breaks through the thin crust, and there starts up a blue flame, as at Paris in communism; but the light is unheeded. Twenty centuries will yet be obliged to look at it. One-fifth of the population of the United States is now in cities, and we had but one twenty-fifth in cities at the opening of the century. The disproportionate growth of great towns is a phenomenon of all civilized lands, and not simply of the United States. London increases faster than England, Berlin than Germany, as well as New-York City than New-York State, and Chicago than Illinois.

This last week in Boston, the American Social Science Association discussed work schools in cities, — a topic not likely to look empty to honest eyes. Much after Thomas Chalmers's plan, there was founded at the North End, yesterday, a biblical and evangelical, but wholly undenominational, church for the poor. It is a good sign. [Applause.]

Boston is now a crescent, stretching around the tip of the tongue of Massachusetts Bay, from Chelsea Beach to the Milton Hills. When you and I are here no longer, this growing young moon will embrace Mount Auburn, and line with its increasing light both shores of our azure sea for miles toward the sunrise. It is, however, unsafe to act upon the supposition, which some seem to harbor, that all the old peninsula here will be needed as a stately commercial exchange, and that the very poor can be crowded out of it, into homes beyond a ferry, or reached only by railway.

The poorest of the poor must live very near their work. We want model lodging-houses for them, like the London Waterlow buildings, which pay six per cent on their cost. For a more fortunate class we must have cheap houses outside municipal limits. But, more than all, we want self-supporting churches among the destitute and degraded.

Boston is more favorably situated than any other American city to show how democracy and Christianity can govern a great town well. First at the throat of Slavery, will Boston be the first American city to throttle Metropolitan Evil?

Chalmers used to affirm, that cities can be managed morally as well as the country-side, if their religious privileges are made as great in proportion to their population.

But, gentlemen, while we embrace every opportunity to call out the efforts of the church in personal visitation of the poor, and in the founding of self-supporting religious institutions, let us not forget the responsibility of the civil arm for the shutting up of the dens of temptation. [Applause.] If you will visit your more desolate quarters in this city, — and the most infamously vicious are not at the North End,— you will find reason to go home with something more substantial as your programme of future efforts than weak regrets, expressed at your fireside over æsthetic tea and your newspaper, about the lack of the execution of good laws here. [Applause.] Seventy-five millions of dollars in this city are engaged in the liquor-traffic; and, if I could shut up the multitudinous doors to temptation, I might shut up the alms-houses. This is so trite a truth, that you blame me for presenting it; but your Governor Andrew used to say, that this truth is trite only because it is so superabundantly true and important as to have been repeated over and over.

You loathe the unjust judges of history; you place in pillories of infamy men whose duty it has been to execute law, and have not done it. Are you safe from such pillories? When we, as American freemen, give in our account before that bar where there is no shuffling, we shall do so as a population to whom the sword of justice was given largely in vain. We the people, and especially that professional class represented here, are intrusted with power, most of which is *not* a terror to evil-doers, nor a praise to them who do well. Under the murky threats of the years ahead of us, it is the duty of the parlor, the pulpit, the press, politics, and the police — the five great powers of these modern ages — to join arms and go forward in one phalanx for the execution of all those just public enactments which shut places of temptation, and leave a man a good chance to be born right the second time by being born right the first time. [Applause.]

THE LECTURE.

Professor Tholuck, in his garden at Halle-on-the-Saale, once said to me, "The Tübingen school, as you know, is no longer in existence at Tübingen itself: as a sect in biblical criticism, it has perished:

its history has been written in more than one language. Only a few years ago, however, we had six broad-backed Englishmen take their seats on the university benches at Tübingen, and ask to be taught Bauer's theology. But Professors Beck and Landerer and Palmer, who oppose that scheme of thought, now outgrown among our best scholars, told the sturdy sons of Britain, that they must seek elsewhere for instruction of that sort; whereupon they turned their faces homeward, sadder, but wiser."

Theodore Parker was a scholar of the Tübingen school. His characteristic positions concerning the Bible are those which have seen battle and defeat of late in Germany. They are perfectly familiar to all who have studied that great range of criticism called the Tübingen exegetical biblical criticism. This had great influence about the time Parker was forming his opinions; and he began his public career by launching himself upon what time has proved to be only a re-actionary eddy, and not the gulf-current, of scholarship. (See article on the "Decline of Rationalism in the German Universities," *Bib. Sacra*, October, 1875.) His first work was a translation of De Wette. In his formative years of study the now outgrown Tübingen critics were his chief reading.

In philosophy, as distinguished from biblical research, we all see that Theodore Parker has founded no new school. His distinctive positions have no large following, even among our erratics. Mr. Frothingham of New-York City, who is one of his biographers, and perhaps more nearly than any other man his successor, said in 1864, in the North American Review, that he anticipates for Theodore Parker as a metaphysician no immortality.

Let me quiet your apprehensions, gentlemen, by affirming at the outset my reverence for Theodore Parker's antislavery principles. [Applause.] Theodore Parker's memory stands in the past as a statue. The rains, and biting sleet, and winds beat upon it. A part of the statue is of clay: a part is of bronze. The clay is his theological speculation: the bronze is his antislavery action. The clay will be washed away; already it crumbles. The bronze will endure; and, if men are of my mind, it will form a figure to be venerated. [Applause.]

What are the most essential positions of Theodore Parker's absolute religion?

1. That man has an instinctive intuition of the fact of the Divine existence.

2. That he has an instinctive intuition of the existence and authority of the moral law.

3. That he has an instinctive intuition of his own immortality.

4. That an infinitely-perfect God is omnipresent or immanent in the world of matter and in that of spirit.

5. That this idea of the Divine Perfection and Immanence is unknown to both the Old Testament and the New, and to every popular theology.

6. That the accounts of miracles in the Bible are all untrustworthy.

7. That, when we are free from the love of sin, we are also free from the guilt of it.

8. That sin is the tripping of a child who is learning to walk, or a necessary, and, for the most part, inculpable stage in human progress.

A very ugly and dangerous set of propositions are these last four; a rather inspiring set are the first four: but all eight were Theodore Parker's. (See WEISS's *Life of Parker*, vol. ii. pp. 455, 470, 472.) Some of his hearers fed themselves on the former, some on the latter; and hence the opposite effects he seemed to produce in different cases. It was on the first four that he not doubtfully supposed himself to have been successful in founding what he called an absolute, or natural religion.

No other document written by Theodore Parker is so important, as an exposition of his views, as that touching, but in places almost coarsely irreverent, letter sent from the West Indies to the Twenty eighth Congregational Society, after he had fled away from America to die. Nothing else in that letter, which he called "Parker's Apology for Himself," is as important as this central passage:—

"I found certain great primal intuitions of human nature, which depend on no logical process of demonstration, but are rather facts of consciousness given by the instinctive action of human nature itself. I will mention only the three most important which pertain to religion:—

"1. The instinctive intuition of the divine,— the consciousness that there is a God.

"2. The instinctive intuition of the just and right,— a consciousness that there is a moral law independent of our will, which we ought to keep.

"3. The instinctive intuition of the immortal,— a consciousness that the essential element of man, the principle of individuality, never dies.

"Here, then, was the foundation of religion, laid in human nature itself, which neither the atheist nor the more pernicious bigot, with their sophisms of denial or affirmation, could move, or even shake. I had gone through the great spiritual trial of my life, telling no one of its hopes or fears; and I thought it a triumph that I had psychologically established these three things to my own satisfaction, and devised a scheme, which, to the scholar's mind, I thought could legitimate what was spontaneously given to all by the great primal instincts of mankind. . . . From the primitive facts of consciousness given by the power of instinctive intuition, I endeavored to deduce the true notion of God, of justice, and futurity. Here I could draw from human nature, and not be hindered by the limitations of human history; but I know now, better than it was possible then, how difficult is this work, and how often the inquirer mistakes his own subjective imagination for a fact of the universe. *It is for others to decide whether I have sometimes mistaken a little grain of brilliant dust in my telescope for a fixed star in heaven.* [Applause.] (WEISS: *Life of Parker*, vol. ii. p. 455.)

Julius Müller, professor in the University of Halle, is commonly regarded now as the greatest theologian in the world. His chief book is a discussion of sin. From first to last, his scheme of natural religion is built with scientific exactness on self-evident, axiomatic, intuitive truth. The very rock on which Parker planted his foot is a corner-stone of the acutest evangelical theology of the globe to-day. Read Julius Müller's discussions (*Doctrine of Sin*, trans. in T. & T. Clark's Library, Edinburgh), and you will find him more reverent than Theodore Parker toward intuitive, axiomatic, self-evident propositions of all kinds. He, however, has cleared the whole surface of the rock of which Parker, in his haste, saw but a part. Instead of building on that broader foundation a slight structure, he has begun the erection of a palace. He has been obliged to stretch its foundations out to correspond in every part with the once unsuspected extent of this whole support of natural adamant. Parker strangely overlooked the fact that we have an intuitive knowledge of sin as a fact in our personal experience. That knowledge must shape our philosophy. Building upon it, Julius Müller did not ask whether the rising walls he constructed would or would not meet, point for point, the walls of the celestial city, which, Revelation teaches, lay in the air above him. He did not look upward at all, but downward only, upon this revelation in the constitutional intuitions and instincts. He explored conscience. He brought to the light the surface of the whole rock of intuitive moral truth, and not merely that of a part of it. He built around its edges after the plan shown in the adamant itself. It turns out, that to-day Germany calls that man her chief theologian, because it has found that these walls, rising from the adamant of axiomatic truth, wholly without regard to the foundations of the floating celestial city above, are conterminous and correspondent with those upper walls in every part, and that the two palaces are one. [Applause.]

It is a solemn provision of the courts of law, that a man under oath must tell the whole truth, and nothing but the truth. In the use of intuitions and instincts, experiment and syllogism, the thing I am chiefly anxious about, is, that we clear the whole platform before we begin to build. We must take the testimony of all the intuitions; we must be willing to look into the deliverance of all the instincts; we must neglect no part of man's experiments, continued, age after age, in his philanthropic and religious life; we must revere the syllogism everywhere. James Freeman Clarke has repeatedly pointed out, that an inadequate use of our intuitive knowledge of the fact of sin in personal experience is a most searching and perhaps fatal flaw in Parker's scheme of thought. Give our intuitive knowledge of the fact of sin its proper place, and, if you are true to the scientific method, the fact that you are sick will make you ask for a physician. I am not asserting the sufficiency, but only the efficiency, of a wholly scientific, natural religion. Every day it becomes clearer to philosophical scholarship, that the whole deliverance of the Works is synonymous, in every vocal and in every whispered syllable, with the whole deliverance of the Word. Certain it is, that the whole list of moral intuitions, of which Theodore Parker made use of but a part, is the basis of the acutest evangelical natural theology to-day. When I compare the structure that Theodore Parker erected here in Boston on a fragment of this adamant of axiomatic truth, it seems to me a careless cabin, as contrasted with Julius Müller's palatial work. What your New-York palace, appointed in every part well, is to that wretched squatter's tenement, standing, it may be, face to face with it in the upper part of Manhattan Island yonder, such is the complete intuitional religious philosophy, compared with Theodore Parker's absolute religion. [Applause.]

What are the more important errors in Theodore Parker's system of thought?

1. It is possible to imagine that the soul is not immortal.

Every materialist here will of course grant me this proposition. I am willing to admit that I think it entirely possible to imagine the non-existence of the soul as a personality after death. The idea of the soul's immortality is, therefore, not a necessary idea. Of course spiritual substance, like material substance, we suppose to be indestructible; but, as a personality, the soul may at least be imagined to cease to exist. I cannot, however, so much as imagine that space should not exist, or that time should not, or that every change should not have a cause. There is a perfect incapacity in my mind to conceive of the annihilation of space or time: therefore it is perfectly clear that the idea of the soul's immortality is not a necessary idea in the same sense in which my ideas of space and time are necessary ideas.

Nor is this idea of immortality a universal idea, as that of space or time is. Some sane men appear to be without any confidence in immortality as a fact; but there never was a sound mind that did not act upon the practical supposition that every change must have a cause, and that a thing cannot be and not be at the same time in the same sense. Your urchin on Boston Common who holds a ball in his hand behind him, and who hears the assertion from some other urchin, that the ball is in another place, knows better. He has the ball in his hand; and he is perfectly confident that the same thing cannot be and not be at the same time and in the same sense. You state that proposition to him, and he will stare at you with wide eyes. He knows nothing of the metaphysical statement: nevertheless, that proposition is in his possession implicitly, though not explicitly. He acts upon it with perfect intelligence. He knows that the ball is in his hand, and that therefore that ball is not anywhere else. This is a self-evident, axiomatic, necessary belief, or an intuition in the scientific sense of the word. Not in that sense, can we call the fact of immortality an intuitive truth.

We have an *instinctive anticipation of* existence after death. We can prove that. There is no real *intuition* of existence after death.

The proposition that the soul is immortal is therefore not marked by the three traits of intuitive truth, — self-evidence, necessity, and universality.

Only a slovenly scholarship could assert that this proposition is marked by these traits. Theodore Parker asserted, however, that the fact of immortality is an intuitive truth. This unsupported assertion was a corner-stone of his absolute religion.

You will, therefore, allow me to say, that, —

2. Theodore Parker did not carefully distinguish from each other *intuition* and *instinct*.

To blunder on that point is so common, that I shall be unable to convince you of the importance of error there, unless you take pains in your libraries to apply these tests of self-evidence, necessity, and universality to a certain class of truths, and see how the tests distinguish that class from every other set of propositions that you can imagine. Only those truths which show the traits of self-evidence, necessity, and universality, are intuitive. Loose popular speech may use the word intuition carelessly; but when a great reader like Theodore Parker confounds *instinct* and *intuition*, and speaks now about our having an intuition, and now of our possessing an instinctive intuition of the immortality of the soul, we must say that he is careless; for it is two thousand years now that self-evidence, necessity, and universality have been used as the tests of intuitive truth. Between an *instinct* and an *intuition* there is as palpable a distinction as between the right hand and the left; and to confuse the two, as Theodore Parker's deliberate speech does, is unscholarly to the degree of being slovenly. I put once before the chief authority of Harvard University in metaphysics the question, whether metaphysical scholars have commonly classed immortality among the intuitive truths. He smiled, and said, "Who taught you that they have?"— "Why, I have read," said I, "that there was once in Boston a religion built up on the idea that immortality is an intuition." And the smile became even broader, although the man was very liberal in his theology. "Theodore Parker," said he, "was not a consecutive, philosophical thinker. No metaphysician of repute has ever classed immortality among the intuitive truths, although it has again and again been classed as a deliverance of our instincts."

3. It is not safe to assert, as Parker does, that the Divine Existence is a strictly intuitive truth.

Pace amantis! Peace to all lovers of the doctrine that belief in the Divine Existence is intuitive! I wish to treat reverently that school of philosophy which asserts that we have an intuition, strictly so-called, of the fact that God exists. To me the Divine Existence is evident; but it is not, strictly speaking, self-evident. It is evident by only one step of reasoning, and is the highest of derivative, but is not really a primitive, first truth, or axiomatic fact. It is as sure as any axiom; but it is not an axiom that God is. I can, I think, imagine that God might not exist. I cannot imagine that space does not, or that time does not. I know that Sir Isaac Newton said that space and time are attributes, and that every attribute must inhere in some substance, and that if space and time are necessary existences, and are really objective to the mind, and not merely a green color thrown upon the universe by the mental spectacles which we now wear, then God must be, for space and time must be. *Pace amantis*, once more! I know how many scholars agree in the opinion that time and space are merely necessary ideas, and not objectively real. They are in the color of the glasses through which we look. The truth is, that recent philosophy more and more approaches the conclusion of Sir Isaac Newton, that space and time are objectively real. Dr. McCosh of Princeton, George Henry Lewes, materialistic though he is, and a score of other recent representatives of rival philosophical schools, regard space and time as mysterious somewhats, which very possibly have a real existence outside our spectacles. They are not simply necessary ideas, fixed colors in our spectacles, but something outside of us.

Now it is true, that, if space and time be objectively real, they imply the existence of something that is just as necessary in its existence, and just as eternal, as they. If they are qualities of any thing, instead of mere colors in the lenses through which we look, there must be a substance that is necessary in its existence, eternal, and absolutely independent; and that can be only an infinitely perfect being. You cannot imagine the non-existence of space or time; you cannot think that they ever were not, or that they ever will cease to be; and so, if they are attributes, they are the attributes of a Being that was, and is, and is to come.

Many are now turning to that philosophy which the later and the older investigation supports, — namely, that space and time are objectively real, and that this fact contains incontrovertible proof of the Divine Self-Existence. But you derive that argument from the existence of space and time; you do not look directly upon the Divine Existence even then. There is a single step of reasoning; and so the truth, although evident, is not self-evident.

I know how many are puzzled to prove the Divine Self-Existence. Paley's argument from the watch, we are told by some who misunderstand it, proves too much. A design proves a designer? Yes. But must not God himself, then, have had a designer, and his designer a designer, and his designer a designer, and so on forever? This inquiry is familiar to religious science under the name of the question as to the Infinite Series. The reply to all that tantalizing objection is, that intuitive truth demonstrates the existence of dependent being, and that there cannot be a dependent without an independent being. There cannot be a *here* without there being a *there*, can there? There cannot be a *before* without there being an *after*, can there? There cannot be an *upper* without there being an *under*, can there? If, therefore, I can prove there is a *here*, I can prove there is a *there;* if I can prove there is a *before*, I can prove there is an *after;* if I can prove there is an *upper*, I can prove there is an *under*. Just so, by logical necessity, there cannot be a *dependent* being without an *independent;* and *I* am a *dependent* being, and therefore there is an Independent or Self-Existent Being. [Applause.]

Thus I must be cautious or modest enough not to assert that we have a direct intuition of the Divine Existence. This truth is instinctive, not intuitive. It seems to lie capsulate in all our highest instincts. Our sense of dependence and obligation, great facts, if barely scratched with the point of a scalpel of analysis, reveal Almighty God, and make the soul's cheeks pale. I cannot affirm, however, that the Divine Existence is self-evident, although it is evident as the noon.

Theodore Parker's assertion that the Divine Existence is known to us by intuition implies that this truth has the three traits of self-evidence, necessity, and universality.

Only a slovenly scholarship can assert that the truth possesses these traits.

On a score of other points, it might be shown that Parker was misled, by not making a sharp distinction between instinct and intuition.

4. He did not carefully distinguish inspiration from illumination.

Once more: peace to the lovers of the doctrine that modern men of genius are inspired more or less — especially less!

There is a book composed of sixty-six pamphlets, written in different ages, some of them barbarous; and I affirm that there are in the volume no adulterate moral elements. It is a winnowed book. Its winnowedness is a fact made tangible by ages of the world's experience. Of course I need not say to this distinguished audience, what Galileo said to his persecutors, that the Bible is given to teach how to go to heaven, and not how the heavens go. Do not suppose that inspiration guarantees infallibility in merely botanical truth. A small philosopher said to me once, "The Bible affirms that the mustard-seed is the smallest of all seeds. Now, there are seeds so small, that they cannot be seen with the naked eye. Where, therefore, is your doctrine of inspiration?" I thought that man's mind was the smallest of all mustard-seeds. Inspiration is rightly defined in religious science as the gift of infallibility in teaching moral and religious truth. The Scriptures are given by inspiration in this sense, and therefore are profitable for what? For botany? That is not the record. They are profitable for reproof, correction, and instruction in righteousness. They are a rule of religious, and not of botanical, faith and practice. My mutsard-seed philosopher, like many another objector to the doctrine of the inspiration of the Scripture, appeared to be in ignorance of the definition of inspiration.

Perfect moral and religious winnowedness exists in the Bible, and in no other book in the world. Is there any other book the ages could absorb into their veins as they have the Bible, and feel nothing but health as the result?

Mr. Emerson told a convention of rationalists once, in this city, that the morality of the New Testament is scientific and perfect. But the morality of the New Testament is that of the Old. Yes, you say; but what of the imprecatory Psalms? A renowned professor, who, as Germany thinks, has done more for New-England theology than any man since Jonathan Edwards, was once walking in this city with a clergyman of a radical faith, who objected to the doctrine that the Bible is inspired, and did so on the ground of the imprecatory Psalms. The replies of the usual kind were made; and it was presumed that David expressed the Divine purpose in praying that his enemies might be destroyed, and that he gave utterance only to the natural righteous indignation of conscience against unspeakable iniquity. But the doubter would not be satisfied. The two came at last to a newspaper bulletin, on which the words were written, — the time was at the opening of our civil war, — "Baltimore to be shelled at twelve o'clock." "I am glad of it," said the radical preacher; "I am glad of it." — "And so am I," said his companion; "but I hardly dare say so, for fear you will say I am uttering an imprecatory psalm." [Applause.]

One proof of the inspiration of the Bible is its perfect moral winnowedness; and there are a thousand other proofs. Inspiration must at least guarantee winnowedness; and I find no modern inspiration that guarantees even as little as that. I am not giving the proof of inspiration, but only illustrating the distinction between *inspiration* and *illumination*.

Why, our literati will probably bow down before Shakspeare as an inspired man, if that phrase is to be taken in the loose, misleading sense in which Parker used it. How often otherwise brilliant literature tells us that inspiration is of the same kind in all writers, sacred and profane, differing only in degree! Very well: if any modern man has been inspired, perhaps Shakspeare was. But is there moral winnowedness in his writings? Shakspeare's father was a high bailiff of Stratford-on-Avon. John Shakspeare, alderman, high bailiff, and justice of the peace, the worshipful, — these were Shakspeare's father's titles; and it was his business to execute the laws. But in 1552 he was fined for the unsavory offence of allowing a heap of refuse to accumulate in front of his own door. The next year he repeated this violation of law (WHITE's *Shakspeare*, vol. i. p. 15). The son afterwards exhibited by fits much of the father's mind. [Applause.] I never read certain passages in Shakspeare without thinking of that experience of the high bailiff on Henley Street, in Stratford. Nevertheless, although Shakspeare's mirror is so wide that it takes into its lower ranges the gutter and the feather-heads, it takes in, also, in its upper ranges, eternity itself. [Applause.] This great soul held the mirror up, not merely to time, but, in some sense, to the Unseen Holy. I reverence him fathomlessly, but not as a winnowed writer. "He never blotted a line," said Ben Jonson. "Would he had blotted a thousand!"

There is no winnowed writer outside of the Bible. You cannot put together out of the world a dozen, or six, to say nothing of sixty-six pamphlets, that shall contain, as the sixty-six in the Bible do, an harmonious system of religious truth, and no morally adulterate element. Where are there six volumes that could be stitched together, even from among those that Christianity has inspired, of which we can say they possess this lowest, and by no means exhaustive trait of true inspiration, — perfect moral and religious winnowedness? The difference between illumination and inspiration is as vast as that between the east and west. Long enough we have heard, here in Boston, that all men are inspired more or less; and long enough have we learned that the confusion of inspiration and illumination with each other may work endless mischief, even when a man as honest as Theodore Parker endeavors to build up, after confusing them, a system of faith.

It is not unimportant to notice that our faith in inspiration, rightly defined, would not be touched at all, even if we were to prove a geological error in every verse of the first chapter of Genesis. I do not believe there is any geological error there. With Dana, with Guyot, with Pierce, with Dawson, we can hold that the record of the progress of events in the creation of the world is correct. If this is correct, it must have been inspired; for, unless it was taught to him from above, no man could have known the complex order accurately of events that occurred before man was. Dana says, in his last chapter of his Geology, " *This document in the first chapter of Genesis, if true, is of divine origin.* It is profoundly philosophical in the scheme of creation it presents. It is both true and divine. It is a declaration of authorship, both of creation and the Bible " (*Geology*, pp. 767, 770). Read Thomas Hill's subtly powerful articles just issued in a book on "The Natural Sources of Theology," and you will find this ex-president of Harvard University, together with Professor Pierce, holding similar views. The biblical record states that light was created before the sun, — a most searching proof of inspiration; for we know now that the first shiver of the molecular atoms must have produced light; and the sun, according to the nebular hypothesis, must have come into existence long afterwards. But what if merely geological or botanical error, touching no religious truth, were found in the Bible, we should yet hold, that, in the first leaves of the Scriptures, we have most unspeakably important religious truth. They teach the spiritual origin of creation; they teach that man had a personal Creator; they show, that in the beginning, God, an individual Will, brought into existence the heavens and the earth. I do not admit that scientific error has been proved against the Bible anywhere; but if an error in merely physical science, touching no religious truth, were proved, inspiration would yet stand unharmed. Parker's trouble with the Bible arose largely from his carelessness in definitions. Confusing intuition and instinct, and inspiration and illumination, he made almost as great mistakes as when he confused the *supernatural* with the *unnatural*.

Call up, gentlemen, that day when Theodore Parker left New York, and put in his Bible an Italian violet opposite the words, "I will be with thee in the great waters." I stood alone at Florence, at the side of the grave of Elizabeth Barrett Browning, and looked on the grave of Theodore Parker. The sturdy Apennines gazed on the soft flow of the Arno; melodious murmurs whispered through the fatness of the olive-branches; there fell in deluges out of the unspeakable azure in the Italian sky the light of the

sun and of the sun behind the sun. I remembered
the culture of Elizabeth Barrett Browning, and her
faith. I could not forget how wide was her outlook
upon the inner world as well as upon the outer,
how subtle beyond comment her instincts and intuitions; and in my solitude I asked myself, which
faith — hers, or his — was likely to be of most service
to the world in the swirling tides of history, and
which the best support to individual souls in the
great waters on which we pass hence. I remembered
tenderly the good there was in this man and in this
woman; but I asked which had the better faith for
service in great waters. Both loved the poor; there
was in each one of these souls at birth a spark out
of the empyrean; and, under that Italian azure, I
asked which faith had been the most efficient in
fanning that spark to flame. It seemed to me, at
the side of those graves in Italy, that Elizabeth Barrett Browning, had she stood there alive, would have
had eyes before which those of Theodore Parker
would have fallen, to rise again only when possessed
of her deeper vision. Strike out of existence that
teaching which has come to us through the God
in Christ, whom Elizabeth Barrett Browning worshipped, but whom Theodore Parker held to be a
myth, or merely a man; strike out of existence that
healing which is offered to the race in an ineffable
Atonement, which in the solitudes of conscience may
be scientifically known to be the desire of all nations;
strike out of existence these truths, — and then, if the
moral law which Parker glorified none too much

continues its demands, you will have stricken out the solution of life's greatest enigma. Great is the law, said Theodore Parker. Yes, I know it is great, said Elizabeth Barrett Browning; I know that the law is spiritual; it is glorious; all you say of it, I affirm with deeper emphasis: but I am carnal; I am not at peace before that law: *who shall deliver me?* Faithfulness to all the intuitions would have brought that man, as it brought this woman, to this supreme question, the resounding shore of our mightiest inner sea; and it would have given assured safety there in the last day for your reformer who disbelieved, as for your poetess who believed; and the safety would have been in this only possible answer: "I will be with thee in the great waters." [Applause.]

IV.

CARICATURED DEFINITIONS IN RELIGIOUS SCIENCE.

THE SIXTY-SECOND LECTURE IN THE BOSTON MONDAY LECTURESHIP, DELIVERED IN TREMONT TEMPLE JAN. 22.

"In natural philosophy there was no less sophistry, no less dispute and uncertainty, than in other sciences, until, about a century and a half ago, this science began to be built upon the foundation of clear definitions and self-evident axioms. Since that time, the science, as if watered with the dew of heaven, hath grown apace: disputes have ceased, truth hath prevailed, and the science hath received greater increase in two centuries than in two thousand years before."—REID: *Collected Writings*, vol. i. p. 219.

"It is well said by the old logicians, *Omnis intuitiva notitia est definitio;* that is, a view of the thing itself is its best definition. This is true both of the objects of sense and of the objects of self-consciousness." — SIR WILLIAM HAMILTON.

IV.

CARICATURED DEFINITIONS IN RELIGIOUS SCIENCE.

· PRELUDE ON CURRENT EVENTS.

IF Belgium or Holland had two kings, we should loftily look down on those European states as illustrations of the effeteness of monarchical government. But South Carolina is twice as large as Belgium, and Louisiana three times as large as Holland, and each of these States has two legislatures elected in our centennial year. Nevertheless, face to face with our wide areas of Mexicanized politics, we loftily foster our pride, or lightly excuse ourselves from political duties, as if after us were to come the deluge. Something of a deluge, one would think, has already swept over us in a civil war; but it fell out of a cloud that was once thought to be not larger than a man's hand. A murky threat in it, indeed; but when that cloud had overspread all our national horizon, when its leagued massive thunders filled all our azure, when its forked zig-zag threats blazed above all business and bosoms, the best of us were yet doubtful whether there was to be much of a shower.

The most popular orator of this nation I heard address a collegiate audience three days before Sumter fell; and, walking to the edge of the platform, he asked, " What is going to happen?" and then whispered, with his hand above his lips, " Just nothing at all."

Perhaps it is worth while to look a little at the murky threat of Mexicanization in portions of our politics; for who knows whether we are to be saved from all our difficulties by an *ex post facto* electoral law? Will troubles never come again? What if a presidential election as close as the last had taken place in the midst of our civil war? Will indecisive contests for political primacy in a territory greater than Cæsar governed never again tempt the gigantic contestants to fraud? Will colossal partisan spoils and political corruption soon cease to stand in the relation of cause and effect? Our fathers studied British precedents to avoid British dangers; but is it not high time to begin to study American precedents in order to avoid American dangers? Are we now seeking to throttle the real causes of our civil distresses, or dealing only with a few of their effects? How long is intimidation to last on the Gulf? How long will the ignorant ballot be a threatening political fact in the slums of Northern cities?

Massachusetts, you say, is very highly cultured, and is outgrowing the evils that attend on the youth of republics. Are you sure, that, when the population of Massachusetts is as dense as that of England, your Massachusetts laws will make every thing smooth here? Has this Commonwealth a right to be proud of its exemption from illiteracy? There are here a million, six hundred thousand people, and a hundred thousand of them are illiterates. Of a hundred thousand citizens in Massachusetts above ten years of age, and of seventy-seven thousand above twenty-one, it is true either that they cannot read or that they cannot write.

The days that are passing over us are serious in the last degree, because it is very evident that our present difficulties — with the ignorant ballot, and with intimidation and trickery in close elections, and with the atrocious rule that to political victors belong all political spoils — will grow. Certainly the perils arising from the ignorant ballot, and from greed and fraud in contests for spoils greater than Cæsar, Antony, and Lepidus fought for, will enlarge as cities grow more numerous and populous, and as political party patronage becomes fatter and vaster.

We may escape from intimidation at last, but not in your generation or mine. There will be, while we are in the world, whole ranges of States, in which it will be at times hardly safe to vote against the will of the governing class, and where a perfectly free election will be the exception, and not the rule.

Lord Macaulay, you know, in letters lately published, though written in 1858, predicted, that, whenever we have a population of two hundred to the square mile, the Jeffersonian and Jacksonian parts of our civil polity will produce fatal effects. You say Macaulay is unduly full of tremor as to the future of republican institutions, and that France frightened him too much with her revolution; but he is exceedingly cautious. Europe has only eighty inhabitants to the square mile; and this historian says, that, when we have two hundred to the square mile, we shall be obliged to manage our politics on some other plan than that which supposes that all problems can be settled "by a majority of the citizens told by the head; that is to say, by the poorest and most ignorant part of society."

What do I want? Am I here to make a plea for aristocratic institutions? Massachusetts has a reading-test: New York has not. It was my fortune, or misfortune, to be born in the Empire State, and it is a grievous thing to me to know that that vast commonwealth, which, above and west of the Highlands of the Hudson, is only a prolongation of New England, is politically under the heels of New York, below the Highlands, and would not be if the reading-test, which my State used to have, had been retained in the popular suffrage. In 1821 our State constitution was revised in New York; and Martin Van Buren, when the reading-test was stricken out, predicted precisely the metropolitan evils which have arisen from the ignorant ballot in New-York City. Eighteen or twenty thousand votes in every municipal election in New York cannot read or write; and they are a make-weight sufficient, in the hands of a few astute and unscrupulous men, to determine the result of any ordinary political contest in that city.

Drop out her twenty thousand ignorant ballots,

and New-York City, politicians say, could, with no great difficulty, be restored to the control of her industrious and intelligent classes. If New York were London, and if her ignorant ballot were large in proportion to her size, not merely New-York State, but, I fear, New England, would be under the heels of the lower half of New-York City.

What are we to do about these things? Civil-service reform is up for discussion from sea to sea; and why should not President Grant's repeated official words on the ballot be also up in this serious time for public thought? In this distinguished audience it cannot have escaped attention that his recommendation of the reading-test in the national vote has escaped attention. President Grant would take the ballot from nobody who has it now. He would let all men who have received the right to vote hold that right. But he would open the school doors; he would cause a common school education to be free as the air; he would make it as compulsory as the summer wind is upon the locks of the boy, trudging his way to the recitations of the morning; he would remove every obstacle to the acquisition of a knowledge of reading and writing; and then, after, say, the year 1890, he would refuse the ballot to everybody who has not learned to read and write. [Applause.] I am glad that Boston does not let this presidential recommendation sleep.

We must be more thoughtful of what is to come in America, or much will come of which we do not think. Which is the more worthy of the culture of a scholar in politics,—to throttle evils before, or only after, they themselves throttle us?

Theodore Parker was a pastor in Boston, and he writes in his journal one day, concerning William Craft, the fugitive slave: "I inspected his arms,—a good revolver with six caps on, a large pistol, two small ones, a large dirk and a short one: all was right." That was efficient pastoral inspection of a parish. Yonder, on the slope of Beacon Hill, Theodore Parker performed the rites of marriage for William and Ellen Craft, two cultured colored people belonging to the society of which he had charge. At the conclusion of the ceremony he put a Bible into the left hand of the hunted black man; and, as some one had laid a bowie-knife on the table, an inspiration of the moment caused Theodore Parker to put that weapon into the man's right hand. He then said to the escaped slave, "If you cannot use this without hating the man you strike against, your action will not be without sin; but to defend the honor of your wife, to defend your own life, and to save her and yourself from bondage, you have a right to use the Bible in your left hand and the bowie-knife in your right." Say, if you please, that all that was melodramatic; say, if you will, that this style of action was Parker's first, and not his second or his third thought. I affirm, that, in the little cloud which we thought had in it no deluge, he foresaw civil war; and that, if pastors all through the North had been equally efficient, there would have been no bloody rain at Gettysburg. [Applause.]

THE LECTURE.

When Daniel Webster was asked how he obtained his clear ideas, he replied, "By attention to definitions." Dr. Johnson, whose business it was to explain words, was once riding on a rural road in Scotland, and, as he paused to water his horse at a wayside spring, he was requested by a woman of advanced age to tell her how he, the great Dr. Johnson, author of a renowned dictionary, could possibly have defined the word "pastern" "the *knee* of a horse." "Ignorance, madam," was the reply, — "pure ignorance." For one, if I am forced to make a confession as to my personal difficulties with Orthodoxy of the scholarly type, I must use, as perhaps many another student might, both Webster's and Johnson's phrases as the outlines of the story. Before I attended to definitions, I had difficulties: after I attended to them in the spirit of the scientific method, my own serious account to myself of the origin of my perplexities was, in most cases, given in Johnson's words, "Ignorance, pure ignorance."

Theodore Parker's chief intellectual fault was inadequate attention to definitions. As a consequence, his caricatures or misconceptions of Christian truth were many and ghastly. I cannot discuss them all; but in addition to his failure to distinguish between *intuition* and *instinct*, and between *inspiration* and *illumination*, it must be said, in continuance of the list of his chief errors: —

5. He did not carefully distinguish from each other *inspiration* and *dictation*.

When Benjamin Franklin was a young man, one of his hungriest desires was to acquire a perfect style of writing; and, as he admired Addison more than any other author, he was accustomed to take an essay of the "Spectator," and make very full notes of all its thoughts, images, sentiments, and of some few of the phrases. He then would place his manuscript in his drawer, wait several weeks, or until he had forgotten the language of the original, and then would take his memoranda, and write out an essay including every idea, every pulse of emotion, every flash of imagination, that he had transferred from Addison to his notes. Then he would compare his work with the original, and humiliate himself by the contrast of his own uncouth rhetorical garment with Addison's perfect robe of flowing silk. He studied how to improve his crabbed, cold, or obscure phrases by the light of Addison's noon of luminousness and imaginative and moral heat. Now, Franklin's essay was, you would say in such a case, not *dictated* by Addison, but was *inspired* by Addison.

Plainly there is a difference between inspiration and dictation. Orthodoxy believes the Bible to be inspired; and her definition of inspiration is the gift of infallibility in teaching moral and religious truth. But, by *inspiration* thus defined, Orthodoxy does not mean *dictation*. She means that the Bible is as full of God as Franklin's echoed essay was of Addison. As in his essay there were both an Addisonian and a Franklinian element, so, speaking roundly, there are in the Bible a divine and a human element; but the latter is swallowed up in the former even more completely than the Franklinian was in the Addisonian. All the thought in Franklin's essay is, by supposition, Addison's, and some of the phrases are his; but Franklin's words are there. All the moral and religious thought of the Bible is, according to the definition of inspiration, divine, and so are some of the phrases; but human words are there.

The chief proof, after all, that the Bible is good food, is the eating of it. The healing efficacy of a medicine when it is used is the demonstration that it is good. Now, the world has been eating the Bible as it never ate any other book, and the Bible has been saturating the veins of the ages as they were never saturated by the food derived from any other volume; but there is no spiritual disease that you can point to that is the outcome of biblical inculcation. We all feel sure that it would be better than well for the world, if all the precepts of this volume were absorbed and transmuted into the actions of men. *The astounding fact is, that the Bible is the only book in the world that will bear full and permanent translation into life.* The careless and superficial sometimes do not distinguish from each other the biblical record and the biblical inculcation. I know that fearful things are recorded in the Bible concerning men, who, in some respects, were approved of God; but it is the biblical inculcation which I pronounce free from adulterate elements, not the biblical record. Of course, in a mirror held up before the human heart, there will be reflected blotches; but the inculcation of the Scriptures, from the beginning to the end of the sixty-six pamphlets, is known by experience to be free from adulterate elements; and I defy the world to show any disease that ever has come from the absorption into the veins of the ages of the biblical inculcation. [Applause.] And, moreover, I defy the ages to show any other book that could be absorbed thus in its inculcations, and not produce dizziness of the head, pimples on the skin, staggering at last, and the sowing of dragon's teeth. [Applause.]

There is something very peculiar about this one book, in the incontrovertible fact that its inculcations are preserved from such error as would work out, in experience, moral disease in the world. Plato taught such doctrines, that if the world had followed him as it has the Bible, and had absorbed not his account of men's vices, but his positive inculcation, we to-day should be living in barracks, and we could not know who are our brothers, and who are our sisters. (GROTE's *Plato*, *The Republic*, "Social Laws.") There was in Plato, you say, inspiration. Very well. His inculcation under what you call inspiration, and I call illumination, would, as every scholar knows, have turned this fat world into a pasture-ground for the intellectual and powerful on the one side; but the poor on the other side it would have ground down into the position of unaspiring and hopeless hewers of wood and drawers of water; and, worse than that, it would have quenched the divinest spark in natural religion, — family life. [Applause.]

Dictation and plenary inspiration are not the same. I avoid technical terms here; but you must allow me, since Theodore Parker so often spoke against the plenary inspiration of the Bible, to say, that, by plenary inspiration, Orthodoxy does not mean verbal inspiration. Franklin's essay was plenarily, but not always verbally, inspired by Addison. If the Bible is written by dictation or verbal inspiration, as Theodore Parker often taught that Orthodox scholarship supposes that it is, even then it would not be at all clear that any translation of the Bible is verbally inspired. If any thing was dictated, of course, only the original was dictated.

In places I believe we have in the Bible absolute dictation; and yet inspiration and dictation are two things; and the difference between them is worth pointing out when Orthodoxy is held responsible for a caricature of her definition, and when men are thrown into unrest on this point, as if they were called on to believe self-contradiction. The fact that all portions of the Bible are inspired does not imply at all that King James's version, or the German, or the French, or the Hindostanee, or any other, is dictated by the Holy Ghost. Even these versions, however, are full of God, as Franklin's essay was of Addison, and fuller. *They, too, will bear translation into life.* Sometimes, as in the Decalogue and the Sermon on the Mount, and in transfigured Psalm and prophecy, it well may be that we have in the original, words which came not by the will of man.

There are three degrees of inspiration; and the

distinctions between them are not manufactured by me, here and now, to meet the exigency of this discussion: they are as old as John Locke. It is commonplace in religious science to speak of the inspiration of superintendence, as in Acts or Chronicles; the inspiration of elevation, as in the Psalms; and the inspiration of suggestion, as in the Prophecies. The historical books of the Scriptures have been so superintended, that they are winnowed completely of error in moral inculcation. But the inspiration of superintendence is the lowest degree of inspiration. We come to the great Psalms, which assuredly have no equals in literature, and which are palpably rained out of a higher sky than unassisted human genius has dropped its productions from. These Psalms, we say, are examples of the inspiration of elevation. But we have a yet higher range of the action of inspiration in passages like the distinct predictions that the Jews should be scattered among all nations, and nevertheless preserved as a separate people, as they have been; or that Jerusalem should be destroyed, as it was; or that there should come a supreme Teacher of the race, as he has come. We find in the biblical record unmistakably prophetic passages, and these are seals of the inspiration of suggestion; for they could have been written only by suggestion. Infidelity never yet has made it clear that the Old-Testament predictions concerning the Jews have not been fulfilled. Rationalism, in Germany, whenever it takes up that topic, drops it like hot iron. "What is a short proof of inspiration?" said Frederic the Great to his chaplain. "The Jews, your majesty," was the answer. If there be in the Bible a single passage that is plainly prophetic, there is in that passage a very peculiar proof of its own divine origin. We have our Lord pointing out the prophecies concerning himself, and he makes it a reason why we should turn to the Old Testament, that they are they which testify of him. Now, if there be some passages of the Bible that contain these prophetic announcements, then the Teacher thus announced is divinely attested, and we are to listen to him.

If, however, we stand simply on the amazing fact of the moral and religious winnowedness of Scripture, we have also a divine attestation. That winnowedness is providential. What God does he means to do. He has done this for the Bible,—he has kept it free from moral and religious error in its inculcations. He has done that for no other book; and what he has done he from the first intended to do. Therefore the very fact of the winnowedness of the Bible is proof of a divine superintendence over it.

Superintendence, elevation, suggestion, are different degrees of inspiration, which is of one kind. But inspiration and illumination, according to established definitions, differ in kind, and not merely in degree; for inspiration, as a term in religious science, —I am not talking of popular literature,—always carries with it the idea of winnowedness as to moral and religious truth.

There is nothing in the intuitive ranges of truth that comes into collision with biblical inculcation; but there is no other sacred book on the globe which those same ranges of axiomatic moral truth do not pierce through and through and through in more places than ever knight's sword went through an opponent's shield. A few brilliants plucked out of much mire are the texts sometimes cited to us from the sacred literature of India, China, Arabia, Greece, and Rome. I defy those who seem to be dazzled by these fragments, to read before any mixed company of cultivated men and women the complete inculcations of the Vedas, Shastas, and Koran. Those books have been absorbed into the veins of nations; and we know what diseases have been the result. *They must be tried by the stern tests which the Bible endures; that is, by intuition, instinct, experiment, and syllogism.* All the sacred literatures of the world come into collision with the intuitions of conscience, or with the dictates of long experience, except that one strange volume, coming from a remoter antiquity than any other sacred book, and read to-day in two hundred languages of the globe, and kept so pure in spite of all the tempests of time that have swept through its sky, that above the highest heavens opened to us by genius, and beyond all our latest and loftiest ideals, the biblical azure spreads out as noon risen on mid-noon. [Applause.]

6. Theodore Parker was not careful enough to distinguish between inspiration and revelation.

By revelation I mean all self-manifestation of God,

in his words and his works both: inspiration is his self-manifestation in the Scriptures alone. Allow me to assert, face to face with the learning of this audience, in the presence of which I speak with sincere deference, that Christianity would stand on the basis of revelation, — that is, on the self-manifestation of God in his works, including the facts of the New-Testament history, — even if the doctrine of inspiration were all thrown to the winds. You have been taught too often by rationalism that Christianity stands or falls on the truth of the doctrine of inspiration, whereas the nature and the degree of inspiration are questions between Christians themselves. Christianity, as a redemptive system, might stand on the great facts of the New Testament, if they were known as historic only, and the New-Testament literature were not inspired at all. Religion based on axiomatic moral truth would stand on revelation thus defined, even if inspiration were given up as a dream. [Applause.]

Will you remember that the configuration of New England is the same at midnight and at noon? It is my fortune to be a flying scout, or a kind of outlook committee, for my learned brethren here, and I carry a guide-book to this delicious nook of the round world; but what if I should lose that volume? Would not the Merrimack continue to be the most industrious river within your borders, the Connecticut the most majestic, the White Hills and the Green Mountains the most stately of your elevations? Would there be any gleaming shore on your coast, where the Atlantic surge plays through the reeds, that would change its outline at all by day or by night because of the loss of my guide-book? Would not north and south, east and west, be just the same? *Inspiration gives us a guide-book: it does not create the landscape.* Our human reason, compared with inspiration, is as starlight contrasted with the sunlight; but the landscape of our relations to God is just the same whether it be illumined or left in obscurity. We might trace out by starlight much of the map. The sun of inspiration arises, and we know the Merrimack and Connecticut as never before; but the sun did not create the Merrimack or the Connecticut. On all our shores the orb of day shows to the eye the distinction between rock and wave; but it does not create that distinction, which we not dimly knew before by the noises in the dark, and by the wrecks.

There is a soul, and there is a God; and, since law is universal, there must be conditions of harmony between the soul and God. *Since the soul is made on a plan, there must be natural conditions of its peace, both with itself and with God; and these conditions are not altered by being revealed.* [Applause.] Newton did not make the law of gravitation by discovering it, did he? The Bible does not create, it reveals, the nature of things. As long as it remains true that there is a best way to live, it will be best to live the best way; and religion is very evidently safe, whether the Bible stands or falls. [Applause.]

7. Theodore Parker did not carefully distinguish

from each other the supernatural and the unnatural.

There are three kinds of natural laws, — physical, organic, and moral. It is very important to distinguish these three from each other; for penalty under the one class of laws does not always carry with it penalty under the others. A pirate may enjoy good health, and yet lose his desire to be holy, and thus be blessed under the organic, but cursed under the moral, natural laws. A Christian, if he is thrown into the sea, will sink in spite of his being a saint; that is, he will be condemned under the physical law of gravitation, although blessed under the moral. We are stupid creatures; and so we ask naturally whether those on whom the Tower of Siloam fell were sinners above all others. Were those who perished in the Ashtabula horror sinners above all others? A sweet singer — one whose words of melody will, I hope, for some centuries yet, prolong his usefulness on this and every other continent — may have been rapt away to heaven in a bliss which his own best poems express only as the spark expresses the noon. But there was somewhere and somehow a violation of physical law, and the penalty was paid. While that penalty was in process of execution, the bliss of obedience to the moral law may have been descending also; and thus, out of the fire and the ice, and the jaws of unimaginable physical agony, this man may have been caught up into eternal peace. [Applause.]

The distinction between the physical, organic, and

moral natural laws, however, is not as important as that between the higher and the lower natural laws. Do you not admit that gravitation, a physical law, is lower than the organic force that builds animal and vegetable tissues? In the growth of the elms on the Boston mall yonder, is not gravitation seized upon by some power superior to itself, and is not matter made to act as gravitation does not wish?

Is it not a common assertion of science, that chemical forces are counteracted by the organic forces which build up living tissues? Has not my will power to counteract the law of gravitation? A higher may anywhere counteract a lower natural law. Scientific Theism does not admit that all there is of God is in natural law. He transcends nature: therefore he may reach down into it, as I, with the force of my will, reach into the law of gravitation. *If he counteracts nature, his action is supernatural, but it is not unnatural.*

Charles Darwin and your Archbishop Butler say that the only clear meaning of the word "natural" is "stated, fixed, regular," and that "it just as much requires and presupposes an intelligent agent to effect any thing statedly, fixedly, regularly, that is, naturally, as it does to effect it for once, that is, supernaturally" (BUTLER's *Analogy*, part i. chap. i., cited as a motto in DARWIN'S *Origin of Species*). According to Darwin and Butler, therefore, a natural law is simply the usual, fixed, regular method of the Divine Action. A miracle is unusual Divine Action. *In the former we see the Divine Immanency in Nature ;*

in the latter the Divine Transcendency beyond it. In fundamental principle a miracle is only the subjection of a lower to a higher law, and therefore, although supernatural, it is not unnatural. (Art. on "Miracles," SMITH's *Bible Dictionary*.) But Theodore Parker taught that "a miracle is as impossible as a round triangle" (WEISS's *Life of Parker*, vol. ii. p. 452), because it involves a self-contradiction. Brought up in the benighted New-England and German schools called evangelical, it never entered my head that self-contradiction was involved in the supernatural; for I was trained to think that there is a distinction between the supernatural and the unnatural.

Mr. Furness of Philadelphia says that a marvellous character, such as our Lord was, must be expected to do marvellous works. We know, that, when men are illumined by the poetic trance, they have capacities that no other mood gives them. There are lofty zones in human experience, and, when we are in them, we can do much which we can do in none of our lower zones. What if a man should appear filled with a life that leaves him in constant communication with God? What if there should come into existence a sinless soul? What if it should remain sinless? What if there should appear in history a being in this sense above nature, is it not to be expected that he will have power over nature, and perform works above nature? Endowed as the Author of Christianity was, we should naturally expect from that supernatural endowment works not unnatural, but supernatural. [Applause.]

It is Parker's teaching that said the resurrection has "no evidence in its favor." De Wette, whose book he translated, affirmed in his latest volume, as I showed you the other day, that the fact of the resurrection, although a mystery that cannot be dissipated hangs over the way and manner of it, cannot be brought into doubt, any more than the assassination of Cæsar.

Theodore Parker, in his middle life, stood vigorously for the propositions which he reached at the Divinity School at Cambridge and in West Roxbury. He was attacked too early. He says himself that he had not completed his system of thought. But he was attacked vigorously; and with the spirit of his grandfather, who led the first charge on the British troops, he stood up and vehemently defended himself. [Applause.] But that early attack caused some of his crudities to crystallize speedily. He was afterward too much absorbed in vast philanthropic enterprises to be an exact philosopher in metaphysics or ethics. He never made himself quite clear in these sciences, or even in the latest biblical research. His own master, De Wette, went far beyond him, and admitted, in the face of German scholarship, that the resurrection can be proved to be an historic certitude. Theodore Parker, although De Wette did not make that admission till 1849, lived ten years longer, and never made it.

Attacked early, and defending his unformed opinions vigorously, Parker's scheme of thought crystallized in its crude condition. *Theodore Parker's abso-*

lute religion is not a Boston, but a West Roxbury creed. [Applause.] It is the speculation of a very young man, besides.

8. Theodore Parker seemed to understand little of the distinction between belief and faith.

He never misconceived Orthodoxy more monstrously than when he said, "It is this false theology, with its vicarious atonement, *salvation without morality or piety, only by belief in absurd doctrines*, which has bewitched the leading nations of the earth with such practical mischief" (WEISS, *Life of Theodore Parker*, vol. ii. p. 497). Gentlemen, is that Orthodoxy? [Cries of "No!" "No!" "No!"] This audience says that this is not a fair statement: I therefore shall undertake to call it a caricature. It is omnipresent in Parker's works. Whether it was a dishonest representation I care not to determine. My general feeling is, that Theodore Parker was honest. He rarely came into companionship with Orthodox scholars of the first rank: when he did, he seemed to be pleased and softened, and was, in many respects, another man. Attacked, he always stood up with the spirit of the drum-major of Lexington under his waistcoat. [Applause.]

What is saving faith? What is the difference between belief and faith? I venture much; but I shall be corrected swiftly here if I am wrong. Saving faith, rightly defined, is —

1. A conviction of the intellect that God, or God in Christ is, and

2. An affectionate choice of the heart that God, or

God in Christ, should be, both our Saviour and our Lord.

The first half of this definition is belief; the whole is faith. All of it without the last two words would be merely religiosity, and not religion. There is nothing in that definition which teaches that a man is saved by opinion irrespective of character. Belief is assent, faith is consent, to God as both Saviour and Lord.

On April 19, 1775, a rider on a horse flecked with blood and foam brought to the city of Worcester the news of the battle of Lexington, in which Theodore Parker's grandfather captured the first British gun. The horse fell dead on the main street of the city, and on another steed the rider passed westward with his news. Some of those who heard the intelligence were loyal, and some were disloyal. They all heard that there had been a victory of the American troops over the British, and they all believed the report. Now, was there any political virtue or vice in the belief by the Tory in Worcester that there had been a victory over the British? Was there any political virtue or vice in the belief by the patriot yonder that there had been a victory over the British? Neither the one nor the other. Where, then, did the political virtue or political vice come in? Why, when your Tory at Worcester heard of the victory, he believed the report, and was sorry; and was so sorry, that he took up arms against his own people. When the patriot heard the report, he believed it and was glad; and was so glad, that he took up arms and put himself side by side with the stalwart shoulders of Parker's grandfather. [Applause.] In that attitude of the heart lay the political virtue or political vice. Just so, in the government of the universe, we all hear that God is our Saviour and Lord, and we all believe this, and so do all the devils, and tremble. Is there any virtue or vice in that belief taken alone? None whatever. But some of us believe this, and are sorry. We turn aside, and, although we have assent, we have no consent to God; and we take up arms against the fact that he is our Saviour and Lord. Others of us believe this, and by divine grace are glad; we have assent and consent both; we come into the mood of total, affectionate, irreversible self-surrender to God, not merely as a Saviour, but also as Lord. When we are in that mood of rejoicing loyalty to God, we have saving faith, and never till then. [Applause.] How can salvation be obtained by assent alone, that is, by opinion merely? What is salvation? It is permanent deliverance from both the love of sin and the guilt of sin. Accepting God gladly as Saviour, we are delivered from the guilt of sin, and, accepting him gladly as Lord, we are delivered from the love of sin. Only when we accept God as both Saviour and Lord are we loyal; only when we are affectionately glad to take him as both are we or can we be at peace. When we believe the news that he is Saviour and Lord, and are glad, and so glad as to face the foe, we are in safety. [Applause.]

V.

THEODORE PARKER ON THE GUILT OF SIN.

THE SIXTY-THIRD LECTURE IN THE BOSTON MONDAY LECTURESHIP, DELIVERED IN TREMONT TEMPLE JAN. 29.

φέρει φέροντ', ἐκτίνει δ' ὁ καίνων·
μίμνει δὲ μίμνοντος ἐν χρόνῳ Διός,
παθεῖν τὸν ἔρξαντα· θέσμιον γάρ.
     ÆSCHYLUS: *Agamemnon*, 1562.

Εἴπερ ἐστὶν ἡ παλαίφατος
Δίκη ξύνεδρος Ζηνὸς ἀρχαίοις νόμοις.
     SOPHOCLES: *Œdipus*, 1381.

V.

THEODORE PARKER ON THE GUILT OF SIN.

PRELUDE ON CURRENT EVENTS.

If every one would mend one, then all would be amended. If every one would mend one, no doubt the union of multitudinous personal efforts would seem to produce wholesale conversions; but these would be only the massed piecemeal results of individual faithfulness. The snows that descend the Alps in avalanches fall out of the sky, flake by flake. If every one were to mend one, undoubtedly there would appear to be some excitement in society. If every one were to mend one, no doubt in the process some mistakes would be made, even by the conscientious. But, if every one would mend one, there would come into society a consciousness of the Divine Omnipresence, and we should forget men, and lose sight of ourselves, in an overshadowing awe of a Power not ourselves. It is an endlessly suggestive fact, that all deeply-conscientious action brings to the actor, and often to the beholder, a sense of the nearness of a Power not of man. A perfectly holy choice makes tangible to the soul the touch of the Unseen Holy. Boston means to do her duty, and therefore already she feels that God is here. While her holy choice continues, that feeling will continue; and, if that feeling continues long, the fashion of her countenance will be altered.

You, men of letters and of the learned professions; you, students; and you, who call yourselves highly cultured, will agree with Cicero, will you not, when he says, that, in the great speeches of Demosthenes, there is always something immense and infinite, and not of man? You are ready to affirm, are you not, with Matthew Arnold, that there is in human history a Power not ourselves that makes for righteousness? Now, if we could live under the fructifying although insufferable light of the scientific certainty that this Power not only was, but is, and is to come, and that it is here; if we could rise up, every one desiring to mend another, and go into society, in the name of Something immense and infinite, that is not of society, although in it, we should be in the right mood to be illuminated of the Holy Spirit this winter in Boston, and so to be useful among the poor, and in the brothels, and in the gambling-saloons, and in the dens of drunkenness.

These places are to be visited. It was no empty bugle-note you heard yesterday on that matter of personal visitation among the destitute and degraded. Astounding as it seems that we are to go into these haunts of vice; women to go into places of infamy to find their fallen sisters, young men into places of drunkenness to find their brothers, middle-aged men into the places where human forms sit as spiders behind the webs of greed to draw in whatever souls can be tempted by the coarser side; however amazing it may seem that these things are to be done in Boston, they have been done in Edinburgh, London, New York, Philadelphia, and Chicago. In the next three months you will see them done here. [Applause.] Some of you will be doing them soon. Immense wants are to be met by immense truths. The law of supply and demand, the commercial principle, is God's law of revivals.

Are there any who think that Boston is learning to rely on scepticism? There is no scholarly scepticism in Boston. [Applause.] In this city, there have been three attempts to found a new religion, and each effort looks now, on the boughs of time, like a last year's bird's nest. [Applause.]

You remember that when Timothy Dwight began his career at Yale College, in 1795, only one student out of the whole undergraduate membership of that university remained at the Lord's Supper. Young men there were accustomed to name themselves after the French infidels. The college was full of unreportable vices. Those were the days, says Lyman Beecher, who was then in college, when boys, as they dressed flax in the barn, read Tom Paine, and believed him. For a long period our land had been full of enthusiasm for France. Jefferson had just come to the presidential chair. There was hardly a leading individual in public life, in his administration, who held what are now called evangelical opinions. President Dwight met a sceptical senior class in Yale College, and they urged him to discuss the question of the inspiration of the Scriptures. He discussed it; he heard them oppose what he regarded as Christian established truth; he urged them to be thorough. He listened to their best attacks patiently, and answered them fully and fairly. For six months he delivered massive courses of thought against sciolism in religious science; and from that time infidelity ran into hiding-holes in Yale College.

Harvard University, yonder, dear to me as my Alma Mater, as are the ruddy drops that visit this sad heart, was as full as Yale of the unrest of this French scepticism at the end of the Revolution. Lafayette turned the whole heart of our people toward France. Young men in Harvard, as often as in Yale, were proud to name themselves after the French infidels. The atrociously shallow and unclean, but brilliant and audacious, Parisian infidelity of the period — a scheme of thought which we now regard with pity, and which no scholar cares to hear named — was then attractive even to scholarly undergraduates. Harvard never had a President Dwight to take the poison of our French period out of her veins. [Applause.] In that fact begins the history of Boston scepticism. This is frank speech; it is not bitter. It is the sad truth; but it will do to tell this now and here, for we have slowly outgrown the poison.

It lay in the veins of Harvard and Eastern Massachusetts all the more deeply, and had the more sor-

cerous effect, because of the half-way covenant which
many Massachusetts churches adopted, admitting to
the communion those who did not pretend to have
entered on a new life at all; and this simply under
the political pressure of the time, or because, for a
while in Massachusetts, only church-members could
vote.

While these powerful evils of the half-way covenant and French infidelity were yet operative, there
was an attempt to found a new religion. And this
religion has had many names, which it would be in-
vidious to mention; but it was always of a liberal sort.
I beg you not to understand me to be in other than
the mood of tears. There is a scholarly liberalism, a
learned liberalism; there is also a limp, lavender
liberalism. It was limp, lavender liberalism that we
had ingrafted upon New England in this sickly time,
when French atheism and the half-way covenant had
prepared the way for the setting of that scion. I do
not see that the grafted bough has produced fruit of
any great importance; certainly it is to be judged
by what it has brought forth. The old boughs are
not only the more vigorous, but they produce fruit
that is more likely to satisfy the fathomless human
hunger for the bread of life. Scholarship has tried
limp, lavender liberalism, and has come to believe in
a learned, large, Christian liberalism that has in it not
much lavender, and that is not limp, simply because
the nature of things on which religious science is
founded is not all lavender, and is not limp at all.
[Applause.]

Boston, in the name of exact science, believes, I undertake to say, that until a man loves what God loves, and hates what God hates, it is ill with him, and that it will continue to be ill until that dissonance ceases. [Applause.] That simple creed taken alone would be enough to empower and equip us for religious activity, and even

> " To put a soul
> Under the ribs of death."

On all sides of us men are living in the love of what God hates, and in the hate of what God loves. I hold it to be incontrovertible, that all clear heads, the globe around, are now united in the conviction, that, until a man acquires similarity of feeling with God, it is ill with him. They are, I think, almost unanimously united in the conviction, that, if a man goes through life cultivating dissimilarity of feeling with God, this prolonged personal dissonance may become chronic, and he may fall into a final permanence of bad character, and this under the momentum of evil habit, and by the simple law of the self-propagating power of sin. That stupendous and irresistible natural law by which men fall into final permanence of character, either good or bad, is in operation around us. We are called upon, joining hands with that law, that is, with Almighty God, to live in similarity of feeling with him, and then to cast ourselves into organizing and redemptive conflict for the deliverance of men from dissonance with God. In the name of tremorless certainty we must proclaim everywhere, that as a thing cannot be and not be at the same time and in the same sense, so, unless a man loves what God loves, and hates what God hates, unless a man comes into affectionate, total, irreversible self-surrender to God as both Saviour and Lord, it is ill with him, and must be so until the dissonance ceases; and that the dissonance is assuredly less and less likely to cease, the longer it continues. [Applause.]

THE LECTURE.

Keep, my friends, the hush of what Hegel calls the highest act of the human spirit, prayer, in this assembly while we ask whether there is such a thing in man as enmity of the heart against God. Theodore Parker said there is not. When the unclean sweeper of chimneys, a dissipated man, comes into the presence of a pure and queenly woman, he understands his leprosy, perhaps for the first time, simply because it is brought into contrast with that virtue of which Milton said, —

> "So dear to Heaven is saintly chastity,
> That, when a soul is found sincerely so,
> Ten thousand liveried angels lackey her,
> And in clear dream and solemn vision
> Tell her of things that no gross ear can hear."
> COMUS, 453.

It is only when a hush, produced by the sense of the Divine Omnipresence, fills the chambers of philosophy, that they are fit places in which to discuss the fact of sin. Not always in Paris has that condition been fulfilled, not always at Berlin or London, not always in Boston. Our ears are too gross to hear the innermost truths of conscience until we feel the breath of eternity on our cheeks. But what a man sees only in his best moments as truth is truth in all moments. As now there falls a hushed sense of the Unseen Holy upon this city of scholarship, it is a fit time to raise the question whether sin is a self-evident fact in human experience. Theodore Parker affirmed that it is not.

James Freeman Clarke, when Theodore Parker was in Italy in 1859, went into the pulpit of the latter, and was so faithful, both to science and to friendship, as to criticise Parker's scheme of thought for not adequately recognizing the significance of the fact of sin. In reply to that criticism, there came to Mr. Clarke, from Italy, a letter, which he gave to Theodore Parker's biographer, who has given it to the world. It is a painful duty of mine to-day to cite this latest and frankest expression of Theodore Parker's views. In his youth Parker had written: "I think no sin can make an indelible mark on what I call the soul. I think sin makes little mark on the soul, for much of it is to be referred to causes exterior, even to the physical man, and much to the man's organization. Ninety-nine hundredths of sin are thus explicable. I am sure that sin, the result of man's circumstances, or of his organization, can make no permanent mark on the soul" (WEISS's *Life of Parker*, vol. i. p. 149).

Were these not the crude opinions of a beginner

in philosophy? Did he hold these opinions through life? Substantially from his death-bed, Theodore Parker wrote from Italy, in 1860, to James Freeman Clarke:—

"Many thanks for standing in my pulpit and preaching about me and mine; all the more thanks for the criticisms. Of course, I don't *agree* with your criticisms: if I had, I should not have given you occasion to make them.

. . . .

"Now a word about *sin*. It is a theological word, and is commonly pronounced *ngsin-n-n-n!* But I think the thing which ministers mean by *ngsin-n-n-n* has no more existence than *phlogiston*, which was once adopted to explain combustion. I find *sins*, i.e., *conscious violations of natural right*, but no *sin*, i.e., no conscious and intentional preference of wrong (as such) to right (as such); no condition of 'enmity against God.' I seldom use the word 'sin:' it is damaged phraseology, tainted by contact with infamous notions of man and God. I have some sermons *of sin* and of *sins*, which I may live long enough to prepare for printing, but also may not.

"Deacon Wryface of the Hellfire Church says, 'Oh, I am a great sinner: I am one mass of sin all over; the whole head is sick, and the whole heart faint. In me there dwelleth no good thing. There is no health in me.'—'Well,' *you* say to him, 'for once, deacon, I think you pretty near right; but you are not yet quite so bad as you talk.

"'What *are* the special sins you do commit?'

"'Oh, *there ain't any:* I hain't got a bad habit in the world,—no, not one!'

"'Then what did you mean by saying just now that you were such a sinner?'

"'Oh, I referred to my *natur*': it is all *ngsin-n-n-n*.'

"That is the short of it: all men are created equal in *ngsin-n-n-n*.

"O James! I think the Christian (!) doctrine of sin is the

Devil's own, and I hate it, — hate it bitterly. Orthodox scholars say, 'In the heathen classics you find no consciousness of sin.' It is very true: God be thanked for it!

. . . .

"I would rather have a good, plump, hearty heathen, like Aristotle, or Demosthenes, or Fabius Maximus, than all the saints from Peter, James, and John (*dokountes stuloi einai*), down to the last one manufactured by the Roman Church; I mean as those creatures are represented in art. For the actual men I have a reasonable respect; they had some spunk in them; while the statues even of Paul represent him ' as mean as a *yaller* dog.' But let *ngsin-n-n-n* go" (WEISS's *Life of Parker*, vol. i. p. 151).

Gentlemen, that is an amazing letter. The tone of it is unworthy of a cultured man, and is astounding in a dying man. Never would such words have been chosen by Channing, never by Emerson, and never by Parker himself, if there had been behind his phrases a calm, scientific conviction that on this majestic theme he was philosophically right. There is in that letter an irritability, I had almost said a vulgarity, of tone, proceeding not from Theodore Parker's better nature, but largely, I think, from his fear that his positions as to sin would not bear the test of scientific criticism, and yet could not be wholly given up without giving up the very Malakoff and Redan of his absolute religion.

Why, if you should adopt as an established truth the proposition that there is not to be found in man any intentional preference of wrong to right, or no enmity against God, and if you should carefully expurgate literature by that rule, how would Shakspeare look? There is no such thing as preference of wrong to right, Theodore Parker says. If there were to be edited an edition of Shakspeare according to this principle, how much would be left of the naturalness of that mirror of humanity? We now have character after character in Shakspeare represented as making evil a delight, and as knowing the right and approving it, and as abhorring the wrong and yet pursuing it. Your Shakspeare edited after the Parker principle, that there never is in man a preference of wrong to right, would be a limp, boneless, flaccid, lavender thing. You would scorn to call such a Shakspeare a fair mirror of human life. You would find such an expurgated edition plentifully misleading in the study of man's nature. In the case supposed, you could not admit that Shakspeare is the prince of philosophers, as well as the prince of poets, and that he becomes both the one and the other simply by holding up his mirror to all that is.

Were you to expurgate the laws of the civil governments of the world according to Parker's rule, where would justice be? Ask the gentlemen who every day stand in courts of justice, and administer in God's name the eternal law of right, and they will tell you, that the expurgation of our courts by the principle that there is no intentional preference of wrong to right would reduce legal equity to moral chaos; and that every thing in law proceeds upon the supposition that man does choose the wrong when he knows it to be wrong.

Where would philosophy be, if it were expurgated

by the Parkerian principle? We have, in the last twenty-five years, studied more deeply than ever before the subjective experiences of the human heart in the moral region. It is coming now to be one of the higest offices of philosophy to ·explore the deepest inmost of conscience, and to reveal to man the extent of that disturbance which must arise in his nature when he loves what God hates, and hates what God loves. It is now the highest office of philosophy to show man not only that he has conscience, but that conscience has him.

I affirm, that, as men who love clear ideas, we do not want either philosophy, or law, or literature, expurgated according to Parker's principle; but do you want theology expurgated by it? Do you want this delicate little shoot you call religious science shut away from the healthy winds of criticism? Is it to be kept behind the walls of some colossal authority, and not allowed to battle its way to its full size in all the tempests that strike it out of the north, south, east, or west? How is religious science ever to become a stalwart oak, throwing out its boughs in every direction, vigorously and graciously, and no fear of tempests, unless it contend with all the shocks of criticism that beat on philosophy and law and literature? Religious science must take her chances according to the law of the survival of the fittest. I maintain, that if you will not expurgate literature, law, and your philosophy, according to the principle that a man never has enmity against God, you must not expurgate your theology according to that principle. [Applause.] We must not play fast and loose with the scientific tests of truth.

Having already shown that Theodore Parker did not carefully distinguish intuition from instinct, or inspiration from illumination, or inspiration from dictation, or the supernatural from the unnatural, or belief from faith, I must further affirm that, he made no adequate distinction between human infirmity and human iniquity. [Applause.]

What are the chief points established by self-evident truths, as to the fact of sin?

1. Moral good is what ought to be in acts of choice.
2. Moral evil is what ought not to be in acts of choice.
3. Conscience intuitively perceives the difference between what ought to be and what ought not to be in the soul's intentions or acts of choice.

These are central definitions, and apprehensible, I hope. Remember that I do not say that conscience knows what ought to be in any matter of expediency outside of the soul. Strictly speaking, there is no right or wrong in external action taken wholly apart from its motives: there is in such action only expediency or inexpediency. There may be physical evil outside the field of motives; but moral evil is to be found only in the acts of choice. Conscience intuitively perceives intentions, or choices, to be either good or bad. Here stands on one side of the will a motive, and on the other is another motive; and, looking on what we mean to do, we decide whether we will do the best we know or not. [Applause.] Right and wrong in motives are pointed out by conscience, and not in merely external action. I do not know by conscience, but only by judgment, whether it is best for me to vote for the electoral bill or not; but I should vote for it if I were in Congress. [Applause.]

There is in conscience the power of tasting motives, just as in the tongue there is the power of tasting flavors. I know by the tongue whether a given fruit is bitter or sweet. No doubt we bring up the fruit to the lips by the hands; no doubt we look at it with the eyes; no doubt we perceive its odor by the nostrils: but only by the tongue do we taste it. So, no doubt, the intellect is concerned in bringing up considerations before the inner tribunal; but, after all, the moral character of our motives is tasted by a special power which we call conscience. This perceives intuitively the difference between a good intention and a bad. But a good motive is one which conscience not only pronounces right, but one which conscience says *ought* to rule the will. Two things are thus pointed out by conscience in motives, — rightness and oughtness. The former is perceived intuitively; the latter is felt instinctively. The *oughtness* is a mysterious, powerful constraint cast upon us by some force outside of ourselves, and operating through all our instincts. I am willing to define conscience as *that which perceives and feels rightness and oughtness in motives or intentions.*

You cannot go behind this rightness and oughtness which conscience points out. Why is this fruit bitter to the human taste? Why is this other sweet? We are so made, that the tongue tastes here bitterness and there sweetness, and you cannot go behind that ultimate fact. You are so made, that, if you do what you know has behind it a wrong intention, there is a constraint brought upon you. You have violated the supreme law of things in the universe. You are in dissonance with your own nature; and there springs up in you, under the inflexible law of conscience, a sense of guilt.

4. Conscience reveals, therefore, a moral law.

5. That law is above the human will, and acts without, and even against, the consent of the will.

6. There cannot be a thought without a being who thinks; nor a law without a being who wills; nor a moral law without a moral lawgiver.

There must have been the thought of the right and of the good before there could have been a law promulgated in the universe supporting the right and the good. That thought of the right and the good, which must have gone before the law, could have existed only in a thinker. The choice of that thinker to promulgate a law eternally supporting the right and the good could have proceeded only from a righteous thinker. There cannot be a law without a being who wills; for law is only the method of the operation of a will. That is Darwin, if you please. That is not Häckel, nor Huxley; but it is Charles Darwin, and ninety-five out of a hundred of all the foremost men of physical science. It is Archbishop Butler too, and Julius Müller, and none the worse for that. [Applause.] There cannot be a moral law without a moral lawgiver.

7. When, therefore, the will chooses to act from a motive which conscience pronounces evil, that act of the will is disobedience, not to abstract law only, but to God.

8. Thus evil becomes sin.

I have defined moral evil as that which ought not to be, or as that which is condemned by the moral law revealed by conscience. Sin is disobedience to the moral law considered as the revelation of a Personal Lawgiver. Sin is a choice of wrong motives. Personal disloyalty to the Infinite Oughtness — that is sin. All agree to this latter definition; but the Somewhat, which I call the Infinite Oughtness, is to all men who think clearly, not merely a Somewhat, but a Someone. [Applause.]

Let us now proceed cautiously, step by step, and convince ourselves that on this theme much may be placed beyond controversy by a simple statement of the acknowledged laws of the operation of conscience.

9. It is incontrovertible, that man often hears a still small voice within him saying "I ought."

Does anybody deny this? I wish to be very elementary, and to carry the assent of your minds point by point; and I forewarn you here and now that immense consequences hang on your admission of these fundamental, simple principles. Be on your guard. Do you deny that sometimes we all hear a still small voice within us saying "I ought"? If a man is conscious of any great defect in his organization, — intellectual, moral, or physical, — he does not blame himself for it; but the instant a man violates a command of conscience uttered in this whispered "I ought," he blames himself. I may have limitations of my faculties, such that I never can amount to much; but I do not blame myself. But, the instant I do what conscience pronounces *wrong*, that moment I know that I am to blame. That is human nature; and Edmund Burke used to say, "I cannot alter the constitution of man." It is in every sane man to say "I ought."

10. It is incontrovertible, that man often answers the voice which says "I ought" by saying "I will not."

You doubt that? Is it not a fact, certified to you by any narrative of your own experience, that you have multitudes of times replied to this still small voice "I ought," by a soft or vehement "I will not."

11. It is incontrovertible, that instantly and invariably, after saying to "I ought" "I will not," a man must say, "I am not at peace with myself."

12. It is incontrovertible, that he must say also, "I am not in fellowship with the nature of things."

Why, this is only tautology. If a man has a powerful faculty within him that says one thing, and another powerful faculty which says another thing, there is within him civil war. Peace ends. He recognizes the condition of the republic of his faculties by his wails of unrest. He knows that the disturbance of his nature resulted from his saying "I will not" to the still small voice, "I ought."

13. It is incontrovertible, that he must say also, "I have lost fellowship with God."

What is there in sin more mysterious than the sense which always comes with it, that the stars in their courses fight against us when we do not say "I will" in response to "I ought"? There is in the inner heavens a voice saying "Thou shalt," "Thou oughtest;" and we reply to that celestial summons, "I will not:" and instantly out of the inner heavens falls on us a thunderbolt. It is by irreversible, natural law that every man who says "I will not," when the inner voice says "I ought," falls into dissonance with himself, and into a feeling that the stars in their courses fight against him. There is nowhere a heart, given at all to sensitive self-study, that does not understand perfectly how the sun behind the sun may be put out by saying "I will not" to the still small voice which says "I ought." *God causes the natural sun to rise on both the just and the unjust, but not the sun behind the sun.* We are so made, that the only light of our inner sky is peace with ourselves. In the nature of things, the sun behind the sun comes not, and cannot come, forth for us, from the east, if we say "I will not," when conscience says "I ought." The simple refusal to follow that still small voice leaves a drought in the soul; for it dries up the sweetest rains from the sky behind the sky. It is terrific, scientific, penetratingly human truth, that the sun behind the sun does not rise equally upon the just and the unjust; and that the rains from the sky behind the sky do not fall, never have fallen, and in the nature of things never will or can fall, in this world or the next, equally upon the righteous and the unrighteous. [Applause.]

14. It is incontrovertible, that he who is disloyal to the voice which says "I ought" must also say, "I ought to satisfy the injured majesty of the law I have violated. Sin creates an obligation to satisfy the injured majesty of the moral law. (See JULIUS MÜLLER, *Doctrine of Sin*, vol. i. pp. 1–200.)

15. It is incontrovertible, that, in the absence of expiation, man forebodes punishment.

That sounds like a theological and biblical proposition: it is simply an ethical and purely scientific one. It is what is taught everywhere in Shakspeare and the Greek poets. It is what is illustrated by all the history of Pagan sacrifices since the world began. If we are to estimate the strength of any human impulse by the work it will do, then this perception that sin creates an obligation to satisfy the injured majesty of the moral law must be presumed to have behind it a most powerful force. Again and again, age after age, it has shown itself to be stronger than love or death. There is nothing clearer than that a man is so made, that after he has been disloyal, after he has looked into the face of God, and said "I will not," he feels that this act has created an obligation which must in some way be discharged to satisfy the majesty and the moral right of the moral law.

It is not a pleasant thing to say that that is the way a man is made; but that *is* the way he is made. A liberal theology is one that looks at all the facts. "Instead of fashioning with great labor a theory that would account for all the facts," Theodore Parker, his biographer Mr. Weiss says, "overcame doubt by a humane and tender optimism" (*Life of Parker*, vol. i. p. 150).

Gentlemen, there must be a philosophy that will account for all the facts of human nature, if we are ever to have a religious science; for whether you will or not think boldly, north, south, east, and west, men by and by will do so, and they will look into all these astounding certainties of human nature. When a man says "I ought," and then says "I will not," he must say, "I am not at peace with myself," "I am dropped out of fellowship with the nature of things," "I am not in fellowship with God," "The stars fight against me," "Nature is against me," "I ought, I ought to render satisfaction." That is the way Nature acts. Shakspeare was philosopher enough to make one of his characters say, when one complained that he was a man whom fortune had most cruelly scratched, that it was "too late to pare her nails now," and that "Fortune is a good lady, and will not have knaves thrive long under her" (*All's Well that Ends Well*, act v. sc. ii.). Even Shakspeare speaks of a "primrose way to the everlasting bonfire" (*Macbeth*, act ii. sc. i.), and of "the flowery way that leads to the broad gate and the great fire" (*All's Well that Ends Well*, act. iv. sc. v.). Too late! Probably Shakspeare meant something by that phrase, and knew what he meant. For one, I think he meant that it is possible for a man to fall into a final permanency of character, hating what God loves, and loving what God hates.

16. It is incontrovertible, that, even after a man disloyal to conscience has reformed, he has behind him an irreversible record of sin in the past.

It will always remain true that he has been a deserter; and therefore conscience will always leave him at far lower heights than those of peace, if he be not sure that some power beyond his own has satisfied the moral law. [Applause.]

17. It is incontrovertible, that, when man is free from the love of sin, he is not free from constitutional apprehension as to the effect of the guilt of past sin on his personal future in this world and the next.

18. It is incontrovertible, that the desire to be sure that the guilt of sin will be overlooked is one of the most powerful forces in human nature.

19. It is incontrovertible, that an atonement may thus in the solitudes of conscience be scientifically known to be the desire of all nations; that is, of all who have fallen into that disturbance of the moral nature which is called sin. [Applause.]

20. The atonement which reason can prove is needed, revelation declares has been made. [Applause.]

I do not affirm, my friends, that by reason I can prove the fact of the atonement. I believe, as assuredly as that I exist, that by reason I can prove our need of the atonement. [Applause.] I do not assert the sufficiency of natural religion; I assert merely its efficiency. I believe that Julius Müller, building on the same axiomatic truths which Parker relied upon, and forming his system with entire freedom, and at last finding it correspondent with Christian truth, has been far more loyal to the scientific method than he who asserted that there is in man no enmity against God. That an atonement has been made you must learn from revelation; that an atone- is needed you can learn from human reason.

Old man and blind, Michael Angelo, in the Vatican, used to stand before the Torso, the famous fragment of a statue, made, possibly, by one of the most skilled chisels of antiquity; and, with his fingers upon the mutilated lines, he would tell his pupils how the entire figure must have been formed when it was whole. He would trace out the fragmentary plan, and say that the head must have had this posture, and the limbs that posture, and that the complete work could have been only what the fragments indicated. Religious science with the dim torch of reason, and not illuminated by revelation, is a blind Michael Angelo, standing before the Torso of the religious universe, and feeling blindly along fragmentary lines. Although the head of this statue is infinitely beyond our touch or sight in the infinities and the eternities above us, and although its feet stand on adamant lower than thought can reach with its plummet, we do know, in the name of the universality of law, that the lines we touch in our blindness in natural religion would, if completed according to the plan which is tangible to us, be revealed religion, and nothing less. [Applause.]

VI.

FINAL PERMANENCE OF MORAL CHARACTER.

THE SIXTY-FOURTH LECTURE IN THE BOSTON MONDAY LECTURESHIP, DELIVERED IN TREMONT TEMPLE FEB. 5.

"Repeated sin impairs the judgment.
He whose judgment is impaired sins repeatedly."
                    BHAGVAT GHEETA.

παλαιγενῆ γὰρ λέγω
παραβασίαν ὠκύποινον·
αἰῶνα δ' ἐς τρίτον μένει.
        ÆSCHYLUS: *Theb.*, 742.

VI.

FINAL PERMANENCE OF MORAL CHARACTER.

PRELUDE ON CURRENT EVENTS.

BAD advice, John Milton says, may slay not only a life, but an immortality.

We have no right to advise the religiously irresolute to any thing which they might die doing, and die unsaved. Applying strenuously to practice that searching and transfiguring principle, from how much dawdling advice should we and those whom we counsel be delivered! [Applause.]

Not a few of us are likely to be called upon this winter to advise inquirers after the religious life; and perhaps some of us will think it sufficient to say, "Read good books," "Converse with pious friends," "Attend church." A man might die doing all these things, and die unsaved. What is salvation? Deliverance from the love of sin and the guilt of sin. Shall we say to the soul which as yet is disloyal to conscience, "Listen to the best public, and read the best printed, discussions of religious truth"? A man might die doing that, and die unsaved. "Attend devotional meetings; throw yourself into those assemblies where the union of many minds and hearts in one purpose, and that the loftiest, makes religion contagious"? A man might die doing that, and not die free from the love of sin or from the guilt of sin.

Of course, you will not understand me to undervalue these tried and crowned instrumentalities for the religious awakening and culture of the soul. They are efficient: they are not sufficient. Nevertheless, many who call themselves intelligent Christians give no other than this dawdling, unscientific, completely unbiblical, and often incalculably mischievous advice to the religiously irresolute.

Will the use of stereotyped religious phrases make our advice sufficient, if it is followed, to save a soul from both the love of sin and the guilt of sin? "Look to Jesus," you say. Surely a man might do that, in the sense in which many understand the phrase, and not be free from the love of sin or the guilt of sin. I do not say that any soul can do that intelligently, and not be saved. What misunderstanding is there of that phrase, and of the hallowed expression, "Come to Jesus"! Some say, "Believe that Jesus is Christ, and you shall be saved. Do you believe that Jesus is God? Then you are saved." I have heard that statement made in not a few inquiry-rooms; but a more infamous disloyalty to both scriptural and scientific truth cannot be imagined than the assertion that salvation comes from merely believing that Jesus is the Son of God. I know where I am speaking, and what I am saying, I hope. It is not unfamiliar business to me to study the holy of holies of a religious awakening; for it was my fortune for some years to act as evangelist, in part; and I have often found in that innermost shrine the most ghastly misconceptions doing immortal mischief. The religiously irresolute must be allowed to rest in nothing which does not involve their immediate and total self-surrender to God as both Saviour and Lord.

Your Romish priest comes to the dying soldier on the battle-field, and there are but a few minutes for religious conversation. Very possibly he holds the crucifix before the eyes in which the film of death is already visible, and says, "Believe that Jesus is Christ, and you will be saved." To witness such a scene many times is enough to make a wise man insane. To misdirect authoritatively a parting spirit not yet loyal to conscience is to slay, perhaps, not only life, but immortality. How does the poor, doubting, weak, trembling soul understand that language? Perhaps he has no other meaning conveyed to him than that, if he believes that God was in some way in Christ, he will be saved. Beyond all controversy, he might believe that, and not be free from the love of sin or the guilt of sin. We read on high authority that the black angels believe as much as that, and tremble. We must beware of falling into the Romish error of confounding assent with consent, or belief with faith. In the name of science, no less than in that of the Bible, we must beware of advising the unconverted to do any thing that does not include immediate, total, affectionate, irreversible self-surrender to God as both Saviour and Lord. [Applause.]

Stereotyped phrases, although struck out originally at white-heat, may, in religious as well as in poetic phraseology, at last, after centuries of use, become cold cinders. Cant is the use of cooled cinders in place of glowing coals. There is as much literary as religious cant in the world. Eloquent as many of our oldest human religious phrases may be, touchingly historic as they are to an educated mind, and measurelessly deep as some of them are to a student, their stereotyped character of course often diminishes greatly their clearness to the head, and vastly their impressiveness to the heart, of the inattentive and half-educated. Once a century, the world needs a new set of phrases for all its greatest truths. Changing phrases for truths that never change keeps the latter always new.

There are two styles of language, — the biblical and the scientific. As a precaution against fateful misunderstanding, why should we not employ both, since our personal interpretation of biblical phrases is often not that which the mind of the inquirer makes? There is a great difference between believing and believing in. I *believe* Congress when it makes a public statement; but I do not *believe in* all the acts of Congress, nor in all its members. I believe Benedict Arnold when he writes an autobiographical sketch; but I do not believe *in* Benedict Arnold. I believe Washington and Lincoln when they write letters; and I also believe *in* Washington and Lincoln. On the one hand we have *believing*, and on the other *believing in* or *on ;* and the Greek tongue makes even a clearer distinction between the two than the English. But when the great words are cited, "Believe on the Lord Jesus Christ," how often, although this language is biblical, does it fail to convey the meaning it always contains, of the necessity of affectionate self-commitment of the soul to God, or of rejoicing personal loyalty to him as both Saviour and Lord? Coleridge said, "I believe Plato and Aristotle: I believe in Jesus Christ" (*Table Conversations*). To believe *in* a person implies admiration of that person's character, and naturally results in confidence, gladness, pride, and alacrity in following his lead.

If in this sense you *believe in* God in Christ, you accept him loyally as Prophet, Priest, and King, or as both Saviour and Lord, and you are learning to love what he loves, and to hate what he hates; and the nature of things will no longer be against you. But until you not only *believe*, but *believe on* and *believe in*, and thus affectionately choose, God as both Saviour and Lord, of course, there is no safety for you, for there cannot be any similarity of feeling between you and God. When you come to believe in him, that means that you love him, and that you are ready to obey him, not slavishly, but with delight. I believe in Lincoln; I believe in Washington: and therefore I am ready to have them for my guides, I am proud and glad to follow whithersoever they lead. If we are to be Christians in a similar sense, we are to believe in God not only as Lord, but also as Saviour.

Shall we look on God chiefly as Saviour, or chiefly as Lord? Which of these infinities shall we gaze on first, if by the gaze the soul is to be transformed into the Divine image?

Two things are meant by the one word "guilt:" first, demerit or blameworthiness; secondly, obligation to suffer the punishment due to our offences. Revelation teaches that Christ our Lord had laid on him our guilt in the latter sense, but not in the former. He assumed the obligation to satisfy the demands of justice on our part; he did not assume the demerit or blameworthiness of our transgressions (HODGE, *Systematic Theology*, vol. ii. p. 189). In the nature of things, demerit cannot be transferred from person to person. Ill-desert rests on the transgressor forever. A criminal who has served out his legal term in prison is freed from all further *obligation to suffer the punishment of the law;* but he is not free from the *demerit* of having been a criminal. He is delivered from guilt in the second sense, but not from guilt in the first sense of the word. A man who has been a deserter comes back to his king, and should receive a thousand stripes. His king takes a hundred in his place, and that chastisement is substituted for the deserter's punishment. The deserter's *demerit* remains; in the nature of things, his king could not assume that. Forever and forever it will be true that the man has behind him the record of a deserter. Even Omnipotence cannot make what once has been not to have been. But, forever and forever the deserter's debt to the law is paid, and its payment cannot be demanded of the deserter. *If, now, that deserter wishes motives to loyalty, what ought he to keep vividly before his thoughts?* his Lord's power, or his Lord's unspeakable condescension? his Lord as his King, or his Lord as his Redeemer? All hearts that understand it, this question melts in this age as it has in every past age, and will in every future age. Let the deserter remember his own irremovable demerit; let him fill his soul with thoughts of his King as his Redeemer.

What am I saying? Look on what God has done: look on what God is. In the old and majestic language, of a depth unfathomable: "Look on the Cross," *and you will lose the desire to sin.* You will find departing from every pulse of your soul all hate of what God loves, and all love of what God hates. Look first on God as Saviour, and you shall learn to choose him affectionately as Lord. *Now, now, now, behold and trust him as your Redeemer, and take him gladly as King.* This is a direction which a man cannot die following, and die without deliverance from the love of sin and the fear of its penalties. So long as you fail to choose God affectionately as both Saviour and Lord, so long your love of sin, and fear of its penalties, will continue; and so long in the nature of things — a terrible authority! — you cannot enter into peace. When you have accepted God gladly as both Saviour and Lord, you, as a returned deserter, can have peace, not *by*, but not *without*, facing the foe. [Applause.]

THE LECTURE.

When Charles IX. of France was importuned to kill Coligny, he for a long time refused to do so publicly or secretly; but at last he gave way, and consented in these memorable words: "Assassinate Admiral Coligny, but leave not a Huguenot alive in France to reproach me." So came the Massacre of St. Bartholomew. When the soul resolves to assassinate some holy motive; when the spirit determines to kill, in the inner realm, Admiral Coligny, it, too, delays for a while; and, when it gives way usually says, "Assassinate this accuser of mine, but leave not an accusing accomplice of his in all my kingdom alive to reproach me." So comes the massacre of the desire to be holy.

Emerson quotes the Welsh Triad as saying, "God himself cannot procure good for the wicked." Julius Müller, Dorner, Rothe, Schleiermacher, no less than Plato, Aristotle, and Socrates, assert, that, in the nature of things, there *can* be no blessedness without holiness. Confucius said, "Heaven means principle." But what if a soul permanently loses principle? *Si vis fugere a Deo fuge ad Deum*, is the Latin proverb. If you wish to flee from God, flee to him. The soul cannot escape from God; and can two walk together unless they are agreed? Surely there are a few certainties in religion, or several points clear to exact ethical science in relation to the natural conditions of the peace of the soul.

It is plainly possible that a man may fall into free permanent dissimilarity of feeling with God, or fail to attain a predominant desire to be holy.

If he does, it remains scientifically certain that even Omnipotence and Omniscience cannot force upon such a character blessedness. There can be no blessedness without holiness; and there can be no holiness without a supreme love of what God loves, and a supreme hate of what God hates. It is possible that a man may so disarrange his nature as not to attain a permanent and predominant desire to be holy.

Theodore Parker, as his biographers admit, must be called a great reader rather than a great scholar. But De Wette, his German master, although most of his works have ceased to be authorities in biblical research, ought to have prevented Theodore Parker from asserting that the Founder of Christianity did not teach that there may be a failure in a free agent to attain a permanent and predominant desire to be holy. Theodore Parker himself ought to have prevented himself from that assertion. In his earlier career he held that our Lord did teach a possibility of the failure of some forever and forever to attain a supreme love of what God loves, and a supreme hate of what God hates. He thought that the New Testament, properly interpreted, does contain in it a statement that it is possible for a man to fail permanently to attain the predominant desire to be holy; and this was one of Parker's reasons for rejecting the authority of the New Testament. But toward the end of his career he tried to persuade Frances

Power Cobbe that the Founder of Christianity did not teach that any will be lost. Parker's writings are self-contradictory on this supreme topic, most of the real difficulties of which he skipped.

It is the wisdom of all science, however, never to skip difficulties. I know how widely intellectual unrest on the topic I am now introducing fills minds that never have been much troubled by Theodore Parker. I know that many conscientious and learned persons have asked themselves the question the disciples once asked our Lord: "Are there few that be saved?" He answered that inquiry very distinctly, "Yes, there are few." Does science answer in the same way?

It would not follow, my friends, even if you were to take our Lord's answer as supreme authority, as I do, that this universe is a failure. All ages to come are to be kept in view; all other worlds. Our Lord's words referred to our present evil generation; and, if you ask the central question in the best modern form, you must answer it in his way. How many, in the present state of our earth, love predominantly what God loves, and hate predominantly what God hates? How many have acquired predominant similarity of feeling with God? Only those who have can be at peace in his presence, either here or hereafter. That is as certain as any deduction from our intuitions concerning the nature of things. As sure as that a thing cannot be and not be at the same time, in the same sense, so sure is it that a man cannot be at peace with God when he loves what he hates, and hates what he loves. There must be harmony or dissonance between them; and dissonance is its own punishment. Dissimilarity of feeling with God carries with it immense wages, in the nature of things. In the name of science ask, Are there few that have acquired a predominant love of what God loves, and a predominant hate of what God hates? We must answer, in the name of science, that broad is the way and wide is the gate, which, in our evil generation, leads to dissimilarity of feeling with God; and many there be who go in thereat: but strait is the way and narrow is the gate which leads to similarity of feeling with God; and few are they in our time that find it. But there are other worlds; there are other ages. "Save yourselves from this untoward generation." Who knows, that, in the final summing-up, the number of the lost may be greater than that of the saved? or, as Lyman Beecher used to say in this city, "greater than the number of our criminals in penal institutions is in contrast with the whole of the population." But I talk of the galaxies: I talk of the infinities and of the eternities, and not merely of this world in which you and I are to work out our deliverance from the love of sin and the guilt of sin, and have reason to do so with fear and trembling.

I ask no man here to-day, or any day, to take my opinions. You are requested to notice whether discussion is clear, not whether it is orthodox. Let us put aside entirely all ecclesiastical and denominational tests. This Lectureship has for its purpose simply the discussion of the clear, the true, the new, and the strategic, in the relations between science and religion.

What are some of the more important natural laws which enable us to estimate scientifically the possible extent of the natural penalties of sin?

1. Under irreversible natural law sin produces judicial blindness.

Kill Admiral Coligny, drive out the Huguenots, permit the Massacre of St. Bartholomew, and you have made a new France. Carlyle says that it pleased France to slit her own veins and let out the best blood she had, and that she did this on the night of the Massacre of St. Bartholomew; and that, after that, she was historically another creature. Having killed Coligny, you cannot look his friends in the face; you kill them, and your kingdom is a new one. When a man sins against light, there comes upon him an unwillingness to look into the accusing illumination; and the consequence is, that he turns away from it. But that effect itself becomes a cause. Keep your eyes upon your Shakspeare, upon your Greek poets, or upon whatever is a good mirror of human nature, and tell me whether these six propositions are not all scientifically demonstrable: —

(1.) Truth possessed, but not obeyed, becomes unwelcome.

(2.) It is therefore shut out of the voluntary activities of memory and reflection, as it gives pain.

(3.) The passions it should check grow, therefore, stronger.

(4.) The moral emotions it should feed grow weaker.

(5.) An ill-balanced state of the soul thus arises, and tends to become habitual.

(6.) That ill-balanced state renders the soul blind to the truths most needed to rectify its condition.

"On the temperate man," says Aristotle (*Rhetoric*, Bohn's edition, p. 70), "are attendant, perhaps forthwith, by motion of his temperance, good opinions and appetites as to pleasures; but, on the intemperate, the opposite."

A man sins against light boldly. To the divine "I ought," he answers "I will not;" to the divine "Thou shalt" or "Thou oughtest," he replies "I will not." The consequence instantly is, that he ceases to be at peace with himself; and light, instead of becoming a blessing, is to him an accusation. The slant javelin of truth, that was intended to penetrate him with rapture, fills him now with torture. If we give ourselves to an exact study of the soul's pains and pleasures, we shall find in man no greater bliss than conscience can afford, and no greater pain than it can inflict. In this stage of existence, the highest bliss comes from similarity of feeling with God, and the highest pain from dissimilarity of feeling with him. The greatest pains and pleasures, therefore, are set over against our greatest duties; and so God's desire that we should agree with him is shown by our living under the piercing points of all these penalties and blisses. But, light having become an accuser, man turns away from it. Then the virtues which that light ought to quicken are allowed to languish. The vices which that light ought to repress grow more vigorous. Repeated acts of sin result in a continued state of dissimilarity of feeling with God. That state is an effect; but it becomes a cause. According to New-England theology, sin exists only in acts of choice; but the newest school of that theology need have no war with the oldest, for the former recognizes as fully as the latter can, that the state of dissimilarity of feeling with God is the source of the evil acts of choice. That state of the dispositions is the copious fountain of sin, and as such is properly called depravity. This state, continuing, becomes a habit; then that habit, continuing long, becomes chronic; and so the result is an ill-balanced growth of the character.

When I hung my hammock up last summer on the shores of Lake George, I noticed that the trees nearest the light, at the edge of the forest, had larger branches than those in the interior of the wood; and the same tree would throw out a long branch toward the light, and a short one toward obscurity in the interior of the forest. Just so a man grows toward the light to which he turns. According to the direction in which he turns with his supreme affection, he grows; and as he grows he balances; and under the irreversible natural law of moral gravitation, — as fixed, as scientific a certainty in the universe as the law of physical gravitation, — as he balances, so he falls; and, according to science, after a tree has fallen under that law, the prostrate trunk continues to be under the law; and, therefore, as it falls so it lies.

Under moral gravitation no less surely than under physical, every free object that falls out of the sky strikes on its heavier side. They showed me at Amherst, the other day, a meteorite that dropped out of the azure; and it struck on which side? Of course, on its heavier. As the stream runs, so it wears its channel; as it wears its channel, so it runs. All the mythologies of the globe recognize this fearful law of judicial blindness.

Go yonder into Greenland with the learned traveller Ranke, and you will find a story among the men of the lonely North, to the effect, that if a sorcerer will make a stirrup out of a strip of seal-skin, and wind it around his limbs, three times about his heart, and thrice about his neck, and seven times about his forehead, and then knot it before his eyes, that sorcerer, when the lamps are put out at night, may rise into space, and fly whithersoever his leading passion dictates. So we put ourselves into the stirrup of predominant love of what God hates, and predominant hate of what God loves, and we coil the strands about our souls. They are thrice wound about our heart, three times around the neck, seven times around our foreheads, and knotted before our eyes. If the poor savages yonder, where the stars look down four months of the year without interruption, are right in their sublime theory as to the solemnities of the universe, we, too, when the lamps are out, shall rise into the Unseen Holy, and fly whithersoever our leading passion dictates.

Greenland says that hunters once went out, and

found a revolving mountain, and that, attempting to cross the chasm between it and the firm land, some of these men were crushed as the mountain revolved. But they finally noticed that the gnarled, wheeling mass had a red side and a white side. They waited till the white side came opposite them, and then, ascending the mountain, found that a king lived on its summit, made themselves loyal to him, surrendered themselves to him affectionately and irreversibly, and afterwards found themselves able to go and come safely. But the mountain had a red side; and it turned and turned, and there was no safety on it, except on the white side and in loyalty to the king at the summit in the clouds. That mythology of the North, lately read for us by scholars, has in it eternal verity, and a kind of solemnity like that of the long shining of the Arctic stars, and the tumbling icebergs, and the peaceable gurgle of the slow-heaving Polar Ocean, far-gleaming under the Boreal Lights or the midnight Arctic sun. Stunted, you think, the men of that zone? Why, on the banks of the Charles yonder, your Longfellow, taking up a German poet, finds the same idea in far less sublime and subtle imagery, and translates it for its majesty and truth:

"The mills of God grind slowly;
But they grind exceeding small."

To me there is in Macbeth nothing so terrible as Lady Macbeth's invocation of the spirits which produce moral callousness in the soul. There is no

FINAL PERMANENCE OF MORAL CHARACTER. 153

passage in that sublime treatise on conscience which we call Macbeth, so sublime to me as this, on the law of judicial blindness:

> " The raven himself is hoarse
> That croaks the fatal entrance of Duncan
> Under my battlements.   Come, you spirits.
> .   .   .   .   .   Unsex me here,
> And fill me, from the crown to the toe, topful
> Of direst cruelty!   Make thick my blood,
> Stop up the access and passage to remorse.
> .   .   .   .   .   Come, thick night,
> And pall thee in the dunnest smoke of hell,
> That my keen knife see not the wound it makes,
> Nor heaven peep through the blanket of the dark,
> To cry, ' Hold, hold! ' "
> *Macbeth*, act i. sc. 5.

That invocation is likely to be uttered by every soul which has said "I will not" to the divine "I ought." It is as sure to be answered as natural law is to be irreversible. Macbeth himself, in a similar mood, says:

> " Come, seeling night,
> Scarf up the tender eye of pitiful day;
> Cancel and tear to pieces that great bond
> Which keeps me pale!   Light thickens; and the crow
> Makes wing to the rooky wood."
> *Macbeth*, act iii. sc. 2.

Have you ever offered in the rooky wood of sorcerous temptation a prayer for blindness? *In the nature of things every sin against light draws blood on the spiritual retina.*

You say that after death you are to have more illumination, and that therefore you will reform beyond the grave. How do you know that you will see greater illumination, even if you are in the presence of it? How do you know that you will love it, even if you do see it? There can be no blessedness without holiness; there can be no holiness without a free, affectionate acknowledgment of God as King, or a supreme love of what he loves, and hate of what he hates. Are you likely to obtain these soon under the law of judicial blindness? You will have what you like; but do you like the light? You have more and more illumination now as the years pass. Do you see it? Do you love it? There are two questions about this greater light beyond the grave: first, Will you see it? second, Will you like it? Unless you have authority in the name of science for answering both these questions in the affirmative, you have no right in the name of science to rely on a mere possibility, on a guess, and take your leap into the Unseen, depending on a riddle. I for one will not do this for myself; and I will not teach others to do so. [Applause.]

Shakspeare has not left us in doubt at all on this theme; for in another place he says, —

"But when we in our viciousness grow hard,
 The wise gods seal our eyes;
 In our own slime drop our clear judgments, make us
 Adore our errors; laugh at us while we strut
 To our confusion."
Antony and Cleopatra, act iii. sc. 13.

Carlyle quotes out of the Koran a story of the dwellers by the Dead Sea, to whom Moses was sent. They sniffed and sneered at Moses; saw no comeliness in Moses; and so he withdrew: but Nature and her rigorous veracities did not withdraw. When next we find the dwellers by the Dead Sea, they, according to the Koran, are all changed into apes. "By not using their souls they lost them. And now," continues Carlyle, "their only employment is to sit there and look out into the smokiest, dreariest, most undecipherable sort of universe: only once in seven days they do remember that they once had souls. Hast thou never, O traveller! fallen in with parties of this tribe? Methinks they have grown somewhat numerous in our day." [Applause.]

The old Greek proverb was, that the avenging deities are shod with wool; but the wool grows on the eyelids that refuse the light. "Whom the gods would destroy they first make mad;" but the insanity arises from judicial blindness.

Jeremy Taylor says that whoever sins against light kisses the lips of a blazing cannon.

I never saw a dare-devil face that had not in it something of both the sneak and the fool. The sorcery of sin is, that it changes a man into a sneak and a fool; but the fool does not know that he is a sneak, and the sneak does not know that he is a fool.

If I were a sculptor, I should represent sin with two faces, like those of Janus, looking in opposite directions: one should be idiotic, the other Machiavellian. But the one face would not see the other.

The idiot would not know he is Machiavellian; the Machiavelli would not know that he is idiotic. The sneak would not know that he is a fool, nor the fool that he is a sneak.

2. Under irreversible natural law, there is a self-propagating power in sin.

Of course, this self-propagating power depends upon the law of judicial blindness very largely, but by no means exclusively. So are we made, that every effect in the growth of our characters becomes a cause, and every good effect no less than every bad one.

The laws of the self-propagating power of habit bless the righteous as much as they curse the wicked. The laws by which we attain supreme bliss are the laws by which we descend to supreme woe. In the ladder up and the ladder down in the universe, the rungs are in the same side-pieces. The self-propagating power of sin and the self-propagating power of holiness are one law. The law of judicial blindness is one with that by which the pure in heart see God; and they who walk toward the east find the morning brighter and brighter to the perfect day.

Of course, I shall offend many, if I assert that there may be penalty that has no remedial tendency. But, gentlemen, I ask you to be clear, and to remember that an unwelcome truth is really not destroyed by shutting the eyes to it. There are three kinds of natural laws, — the physical, the organic, and the moral. *I affirm that " Never too late to mend " is not a doctrine of science in the domain of the physical laws, nor is it in that of the organic.*

Under the physical laws of gravitation a ship may careen to the right or left, and only a remedial effect be produced. The danger may teach the crew seamanship; it makes men bold and wise. Thus the penalty of violating, up to a certain point, the physical law, is remedial in its tendency. But let the ship careen beyond a certain line, and it capsizes. If it be of iron, it remains at the bottom of the sea; and hundreds and hundreds of years of suffering of that penalty has no tendency to bring it back. Under the physical natural laws, plainly there is such a thing as its being too late to mend. In their immeasurable domain there is a distinction between penalty that has a remedial tendency, and penalty that has no remedial tendency at all.

So, under the organic law, your tropical tree, gashed at a certain point, may throw forth its gums, and even have greater strength than before; but gashed beyond the centre, cut through, the organic law is so far violated, that the tree falls; and after a thousand years you do not expect to see the tree escape from the dominion of the law which is enforcing upon it penalty, do you? There is no tendency in that penalty toward remedial effect; none at all; and you know it. Therefore, under the organic laws, there is such a thing as its being too late to mend.

Now, gentlemen, keep your eyes fastened upon the great principle of analogy, which Newton and Butler call the supreme rule in science, and ask yourselves whether, if you were to find some strange animal in a geological stratum, and if you were to know, by having one of its hands free, that it had three fingers, and if you were to find two fingers on the other hand free from the rock, and both shutting toward the palm, you would not infer that the third finger, if you could loosen it from the rock, would also be found closing toward the palm? Just so, I ask, whether, if we find, that, under two sets of natural laws which are all included under three classes, there is incontrovertibly such a thing as penalty without remedial effect, may there not be the same under the third set? Two fingers shut towards the palm. I cannot quite trace the whole range of the moral law; but I know by analogy, that, if two fingers shut towards the palm, the third probably does. *If there is such a thing as its being forever too late to mend under the organic and the physical natural law, probably, and more than probably, there is such a thing under the moral natural law.* [Applause.]

Yes; but you say the will is free, and therefore that it cannot be supposed that a man will fall into final dissimilarity of feeling with God, or can so lose the desire to be holy, that he will not choose the right when greater light comes. You affirm that the self-propagating power of sin may place necessity upon the disordered nature. You say that the denial that all moral penalty is remedial requires us to deny that the will of lost souls continues free. I beg your pardon again, and that in the name of science. Gentlemen, there may be certainty where there is no necessity.

Is John Milton putting together a self-contradiction

when he pictures Satan as making evil his good, and as yet retaining a free will? Is he uttering self-contradiction when he shows us a fiendish character which retains yet some elements of its original brightness? Has Milton's Satan lost free will? I affirm that you know that John Milton's Satan is not an impossible character. You say you do not care what Milton says; but I am not asking you to accept his theology. Let me not be misunderstood in my citations of the poets as witnesses to what man is. Paradise Lost is a great classic; and no poem attains that rank if it is full of manifest absurdities. Now, Milton's Satan is a character in which the disarrangement of the soul is supposed to have become permanent; he has fallen into final permanence of evil character; and yet he is represented as absolutely free, and not very near annihilation. I appeal to classical literature to show that a permanent evil character with a free will is not a psychological self-contradiction. You admit this readily, age after age, in your great classics; but the instant I here, standing face to face with natural religion, assert that there may be a final permanence of free character, bad as well as good, and good as well as bad, you stand aghast at your own proceeding. Gentlemen, you and I must have no cross-purposes with the nature of things. If Milton's description is not a psychological self-contradiction, there may be a person of permanently bad character, absolutely free, and therefore responsible. [Applause.]

Origen used to teach that the prince of fiends

might return to a glad allegiance to God; and so did Robert Burns, whom Emerson commends for using these words, originally written to attack the proposition I am now defending, but, after all, containing most subtle confirmation of it:

> "Auld Nickie Ben,
> An' wad ye tak a thought and men',
> Ye aiblins might — I dinna ken —
> Still hae a stake."

No, gentlemen; the self-propagating power of sin may produce a state of soul in which evil is chosen as good, and in which it is forever too late to mend, and yet not destroy free will.

3. *Under irreversible natural law character tends to a final permanence, good or bad. In the nature of the case, a final permanence is attained but once.*

If asked whether final permanence of character is a natural law, what should you say, if we were to speak without reference to conclusions in religious science? How have men in all ages expressed themselves in literature and philosophy on this theme? Is it not perfectly certain that all the great writers of the world justify the proposition that character tends to a final permanence, good or bad?

Gentlemen, this universe up to the edge of the tomb is not a joke. There are in this life serious differences between the right hand and the left. Nevertheless, in our present career, a man has but one chance. Even if you come weighted into the world, as Sindbad was with the Old Man of the Sea, you have but one chance. Time does not fly in a circle, but forth, and right on. The wandering, squandering, desiccated moral leper is gifted with no second set of early years. There is no fountain in Florida that gives perpetual youth; and the universe might be searched, probably, in vain for such a spring. Waste your youth; in it you shall have but one chance. Waste your middle life; in it you shall have but one chance. Waste your old age; in it you shall have but one chance. It is an irreversible natural law that character attains final permanence, and in the nature of things final permanence can come but once. This world is fearfully and wonderfully made, and so are we, and we shall escape neither ourselves nor these stupendous laws. It is not to me a pleasant thing to exhibit these truths from the side of terror; but, on the other side, these are the truths of bliss; for, by this very law through which all character tends to become unchanging, a soul that attains a final permanence of good character runs but one risk, and is delivered once for all from its torture and unrest. [Applause.] It has passed the bourn from behind which no man is caught out of the fold. He who is the force behind all natural law is the keeper of his sheep, and no one is able to pluck them out of his hand. Himself without variableness or shadow of turning, he maintains the irreversibleness of all natural forces, one of which is the insufferably majestic law by which character tends to assume final permanence, good, as well as bad.

4. Under irreversible natural law there may be in

the soul a permanent failure to attain a predominant and enduring desire to be holy.

With incisive scientific clearness, Julius Müller says, "*Such is the constitution of things that unwillingness to goodness may ripen into eternal voluntary opposition to it*" (*Doctrine of Sin*, vol. ii.).

The inveteracy of sin! have you ever heard of that? Out of its acknowledged inveteracy will *not* easily arise its evanescence. Out of its prolongation comes its inveteracy, and out of its inveteracy may come its permanence.

Here and now I do not touch the topic of the annihilation of those who fall into permanent dissimilarity of feeling with God; for I do not see that this cause produces any tendency to annihilation in this world, when a man becomes incorrigibly bad. Villains do not commonly lack force. Your Nero, with his murders and leprosies, has put his nature out of order; but look at his evil face in marble on the Capitoline Hill, and you start as if gazing into a demon's eyes. He is as little weak as a volcano. What do men mean when they talk of vice annihilating souls? It disarranges them; but disarrangement is not annihilation. Tacitus says that Nero heard the sound of a trumpet and groans from the grave of his mother Agrippina whom he had murdered. His disarrangement was not derangement. Acting fitfully, all the wheels of the faculties continued to exist in Nero; and they are none of them without movement. They grind on each other, no doubt; but I do not find that spiritual wheels can be pulverized. Do you know how they can be? This idea that evil is to annihilate us ought to have some distinctly scientific support in the experience of this life.

5. Under irreversible natural law there may exist in the universe eternal sin.

It is not my duty here to expound the Scriptures; but you will allow me to say, gentlemen, that "eternal sin" is a scriptural phrase. As all these scholars know, we must read in the twenty-ninth verse of the third chapter of Mark, *hamartematos*, and not *kriseos*. He who sinneth against the Holy Ghost is in danger of "*eternal sin*." Theodore Parker used to say that the profoundest expressions in the New Testament are those which are most likely to have been correctly reported. What phrase on this theme is profounder than "eternal sin"? Dean Alford well says, that "it is to the critical treatment of the sacred text, that we owe the restoration of such important and deep-reaching expressions as this." Lange calls it "a strong and pregnant expression."

It is not the best way in which to teach the truth of future punishment, to say that a man is punished forever and forever for the sins of that hand's-breadth of duration we call time. If the soul does not repent of these with contrition, and not merely with attrition, the nature of things forbids its peace. But the Biblical and the natural truth is, that prolonged dissimilarity of feeling with God may end in eternal sin. If there is eternal sin, there will be eternal punishment. Final permanence of character under the laws of judicial blindness and the self-propagating power of sin is the truth emphasized by both God's word and his works.

6. Under irreversible natural law there can be no blessedness without holiness.

Here I leave you face to face with the nature of things, the authority which dazzled Socrates. God's Omnipotence cannot force blessedness on a soul that has lost the predominant desire to be holy. Omniscience cannot make happy a man who loves what God hates, and hates what God loves. If you fall into predominant dissimilarity of feeling with God, it is out of his power to give you blessedness. Undoubtedly we are, of all men, most miserable, unless, with our deliverance from the guilt of sin, there comes to us also deliverance from the love of it. Without holiness there can be no blessedness; but there can be no holiness without a predominant love of what God loves, and hate of what God hates. We grow wrong; we allow ourselves to crystallize in habits that imply a loss of the desire to be holy; and at last, having made up our minds not to love predominantly what God loves, and hate what he hates, we are amazed that we have not blessedness. But the universe is not amazed. The nature of things is but another name for the Divine Nature. God would not be God if there could be blessedness without holiness. [Applause.]

VII.

CAN A PERFECT BEING PERMIT EVIL?

THE SIXTY-FIFTH LECTURE IN THE BOSTON MONDAY LECTURESHIP, DELIVERED IN TREMONT TEMPLE FEB. 12.

"Prope est a te Deus, tecum est, intus est! ita dico, Lucili: sacra inter nos spiritus sedet, malorum bonorumque nostrorum observator et custos: hic, prout a nobis tractatus est, ita nos ipse tractat." — SENECA.

"Dieu nous veult apprendre que les bons ont autre chose à esperer, et les mauvais autre chose à craindre, que les fortunes ou infortunes de ce monde." — MONTAIGNE.

VII.

CAN A PERFECT BEING PERMIT EVIL?

PRELUDE ON CURRENT EVENTS.

BEFORE landing on the surly Massachusetts shore, our fathers, in the cabin of the Mayflower, drew up a civil compact. It opens with a sentence which Daniel Webster used to say is really the first clause in the Constitution of the United States: "In the name of God, Amen." There are now in this yet young nation church-members enough, including the Romish, to constitute one in six of the entire population. It would appear that this first clause of the Constitution would be good for something, if church-members were good for any thing. In 1800 we had only one in fifteen inside the church.

Professor Tholuck, with the emphasis of tears in his deep, spiritual eyes, once said to me at Halle, in his garden on the banks of the Saale, that he regretted nothing so much in the arrangements of the German state churches as that the distinction between the converted and the unconverted, which Whitefield and Jonathan Edwards drew so deeply upon the mind of New England, is almost unknown, not to the theories, but to the church practices, of Germany. "We are all mixed pell-mell together," said he. "After confirmation, we are all, in one sense, members of the church. I have always regarded the distinction you preserve in New England between a man who has made a solemn public profession of his purpose to lead a religious life, and the one who has not, as the most important portion of the unwritten constitution of your nation." Except Scotland, there is no land on the globe that makes as much of this distinction as New England does. So has the spirit of the unwritten law permeated society at large here and in Scotland, that disgusts of the world with the church are sure to stifle the usefulness of the latter, if this law is administered laxly.

Whitefield often affirmed that he would rather have a church with ten men in it right with God than one with five hundred at whom the world laughs in its sleeves. Not long ago, I heard of a church-member who had failed four times, and paid only ten cents on the dollar, and who had three times assigned his property to relatives in an infamous manner. He was making a speech in a summer evening devotional gathering; and the shutters of the basement of the church were open, and the quick, sharp boys of the common were within hearing. This religious man was saying, "I am of the opinion that our congregation should all alone maintain a missionary on some foreign shore. For such a purpose I will myself give a hundred dollars." — "Ten cents on the dollar?" said a boy outside the shutters of a window. [Applause.] Now, what if that boy had been placed face to face with that man for conversation on personal religion? You say this is an extreme case; but, under our voluntary system, which, no doubt, teaches us religious activity and generosity, there will be, as our population grows, cases like this arising with alarming frequency in great towns, where men cannot watch each other, although they are members of the same church. Your voluntary system has priceless effects; but one of its incidental disadvantages is, that, unless a spirit of most uncommon piety pervades and fires the church, you cannot shut out the dross you would not have, while you take in the gold you must have. Judas, in your voluntary church-system, often carries the bag; often, I say, not always; and sometimes, when he does carry it, the infelicity is, that he rules the purse-strings, and will not go and hang himself. [Applause.] What is the chief difficulty in such conversations as we are many of us sure to be asked this winter to enter into with the unconverted? Hands not clean in business; ledgers that will not bear a neighbor's glance; a personal record behind the church-member which he dares not open to the world; or, in brief, any lack of crystallineness that prevents the transmission of God's light through you. If we are indeed open to all the influences of conscience as the air is to the light, then, when the radiance of the sky behind the sky shines on us, it will shine through us; and it will be found that God's sunbeams will in such a sense penetrate us, that through us men may look into his face. But there are smutched windows, on the panes of which the soot and grime of city greed and fraud have fallen flake by flake. Who cares to look through them toward God? That kind of dim religious light is not of the devoutest sort; and the world knows the fact.

No doubt, the disgusts of the world with the church are many of them unjustifiable; and particularly is it improper for the pulpit to be called upon to be as brilliant twice or thrice a week as the lecture platform is once a year. We ask our ministry to perform arduous parish duties, and to be brilliant orators besides, three times or twice a week before the same audience, year after year. No such task is put upon any lecturer or upon any congressman. As matters stand, I think the average sermon is intellectually as able as the average congressional speech. You cannot have a Burke or Shakspeare in every editor's chair; but pulpits are more numerous than newspapers. If, therefore, you think it natural that some of our newspapers should be the weakest of weeklies, and if some of them are conducted by men who make portions of our press lineal descendants of the reptiles that filled old Egypt, what must we say when pulpits, more numerous than editors' chairs, must all be filled by men who have character? The American ministry, for intellectual equipment and general intellectual capacity, assuredly compares favorably with any other the world ever saw, and with any profession of equal numbers.

But the world has a right to be disgusted if moral faults in the church sow the soil of religious society with the bowlders of distrust. When we cast in the ploughshare, when we try to turn up to God's noon the soil of New England to-day, we meet yet with bowlders enough beneath the soil. Some prayer-meetings you cannot get young men into any more than you can a rat into a trap without a bait; and the reason is, that business-men are there who have no good record with society. Give me but a few princes in business, who are also princes in the church, — and there are some such princes in Boston; they are not infrequently found throughout New England, although their names are infrequently heralded, — give me princes among men, and I will give you princes who can set religious fashions of the divine sort easily.

What are the chief parts of the religious conversation which the religiously resolute should hold with the religiously irresolute? I think four things should occur in every religious conversation of this endlessly sacred sort. First, let there be secret prayer on your part, of the kind that approaches God through total, affectionate, irreversible self-surrender to conscience; and this act will permeate you, by fixed natural law, with a strange power not your own. Unless you know how to obtain an equipment of entire genuineness, beware how you approach any human being on religious topics. Next ask the person you converse with, "What is your chief religious difficulty?" It is vastly important to avoid debate in such secret moments, and it is yet more vastly important to turn all thoughts upon the deepest inmost of conscience. This question I, for one, have found, in somewhat more than a hand's breadth of experience, quite as useful as any other in effecting both these objects. Perhaps the man with whom you converse does not know what his greatest difficulty is; but, if you induce him to make an effort to state that difficulty, you will help him to solve it. Difficulty well stated is half solved. "What is the knot that chokes you?" Perhaps he thinks of some secret sin of his own; and thinks, also, that you have a greater secret sin. If he thinks this, you will not untie the knot; perhaps he may untie yours. Nothing so stimulates a dead man as to set him at the work of reviving the dead. [Applause.] Try, next, to untie the knot by clear ideas and sound words. Then, lastly, kneel down with that man, and, by the contagious self-surrender of two souls face to face with the Unseen Holy, ask the Divine Nature to untie the knot.

Give me a complete self-surrender of the will to God as both Saviour and Lord, and there is no knot that will not be untied in time. Indeed, whoever will untie that supreme knot of dissimilarity of feeling with God which now chokes us all, will find that he has done something strangely strategic; he has brought into his service the law of the self-propagating power of divine affections; and little by little he will be taken into the fold, from behind which no force, human or infernal, has power to snatch him out. Nay, not little by little! On the instant of total self-surrender, the kneeling man may be crowned, or may have given him from on high a new, supreme passion. If he be really genuine in his self-surrender to God, there will, at the instant of such surrender, spring up in him a new life, consisting of a predominant love of what God loves, and a predominant hate of what God hates. Thus the drunkard will lose his thirst, as he cannot under any resolution of a merely secular sort. Thus, as a supreme miracle, she who might be queenly, she who had a mother pure as yours was, she whom you tread into the mire, she whom natural instincts of her own sex are the swiftest and none too swift to condemn, may have given her of Almighty God at the instant of her total and glad surrender to him, though never till then, the kiss which awaits a returning prodigal sister; and, after his kiss, deserve yours. [Applause.]

THE LECTURE.

In the Singalese books of Gotama Buddha, written under the shadow of the Himalayas, we find the statement, that as surely as the pebble cast heavenward abides not there, but returns to the earth, so, proportionate to thy deed, good or ill, will the desire of thy heart be meted out to thee in whatever form or world thou shalt enter. It was the opinion of Socrates, recorded with favor by Plato, that "the wicked would be too well off if their evil deeds came to an end" (JOWETT's *Plato, Introduction to Phædo*).

All disloyalty to the still small voice which declares what ought to be is followed by pain. *What if it were not?* Is God God, if, with unscientific liberalism, we in our philosophy put the throne of the universe upon rockers, and make of it an easy-chair from which lullabys are sung both to the evil and to the good?

Whatever we do, God is on our side! So say many who would not dare to affirm, that, whatever we do, the nature of things is on our side. But the nature of things is only the total outcome of the requirements of the perfections of the Divine Nature. God is behind the nature of things; and you and I cannot trifle with him any more than with it. He was; he is; he is to come. It was; it is; it is to come. It is he.

Great literature always recognizes the law of moral gravitation. Seeking the deepest modern words, I open, for instance, Thomas Carlyle, and read:

"'Penalties:' quarrel not with the old phraseology, good reader; attend, rather, to the thing it means. The word was heard of old, with a right solemn meaning attached to it, from theological pulpits and such places, and may still be heard there, with a half meaning, or with no meaning, though it has rather become obsolete to modern ears. But the *thing* should not have fallen obsolete: the thing is a grand and solemn truth, expressive of a silent law of heaven, which continues forever valid. The most untheological of men may still assert the thing, and invite all men to notice it as a silent monition and prophecy in this Universe, to take it, with more of awe than they are wont, as a correct reading of the Will of the Eternal in respect of such matters, and in their modern sphere to bear the same well in mind.

"The want of loyalty to the Maker of this universe!—he who wants that, what else has he, or can he have? If you do not, you Man or you Nation, love the Truth enough, but try to make a chapman-bargain with Truth, instead of giving yourself wholly, soul and body and life to her, Truth will not live with you, Truth will depart from you; and only Logic, 'Wit' (for example, 'London Wit'), Sophistry, Virtu, the Æsthetic Arts, and perhaps (for a short while) Book-keeping by double entry, will abide with you. You will follow falsity, and think it truth, you unfortunate Man or Nation. You will, right surely, you for one, stumble to the Devil; and are every day and hour, little as you imagine it, making progress thither" (CARLYLE, *Frederick the Great*, vol. i. pp. 270, 271).

This majestic keynote of scientific, ethical truth is the deep tone that leads the anthem of all great thought since the world began. Open, now, Theodore Parker; and how harshly his words clash with Carlyle's!

"The infinite perfection of God is the corner-stone of all my theological and religious teaching, the foundation, perhaps, of all that is peculiar in my system. It is not known to the Old Testament or the New; it has never been accepted by any sect in the Christian world. The idea of God's imperfection has been carried out with dreadful logic in the Christian scheme. In the ecclesiastical conception of the Deity there is a fourth person in the Godhead,— namely, the Devil,— an outlying member, unacknowledged, indeed, the complex of all evil, but as much a part of Deity as either Son or Holy Ghost, and far more powerful than all the rest, who seem but jackals to provide for this roaring lion" (WEISS, *Life of Parker*, vol. ii. p. 470).

"God is a perfect Creator, making all from a perfect motive, for a perfect purpose. The motive must be love, the purpose welfare. The perfect Creator is a perfect Providence, love becoming a universe of perfect welfare." (*Ibid.*, p. 471.)

"Optimism is the religion of science." "*Every fall is a fall upward.*" (*Sermons on Theism*, p. 408. See also pp. 147 and 299.)

One feels, in reading Theodore Parker, that, whatever we do, God is on our side. Carlyle is of a very different opinion. He is moved by no faith deeper than that the distinction between duty and its opposite is "quite infinite." What is in the lines here in Parker is not so painful as what is between the lines. Place side by side this free-thinker Carlyle, and that free-thinker Parker, and ask which is the truer of the two to the deep intuitions of the soul. Contrast the seriousness of Buddha, and the tone of this man of Massachusetts Bay. Compare Socrates and Plato under the shade of the Acropolis, with this modern man under the shade of — what? Of a stunted mental philosophy, rooted well, indeed, in our soil in his time, but only a very imperfect growth as yet, and hardly risen above the ground, when the attempt was made here to deny the existence of sin, and of its natural wages in the universe in the name of an intuitive philosophy, which asserts precisely the opposite in both cases. [Applause.]

Of course, gentlemen, you expect me not to skip the topic of the origin of evil; for, after all, the question which touches that theme quite as often as any other drives men into intellectual unrest, throwing some into atheism, some into a denial of the authority of Scripture, some into various forms of a false, loose, unscholarly liberalism.

CAN A PERFECT BEING PERMIT EVIL? 177

What are the more important points which the use of the scientific method can make clear on this multiplex, overawing theme of the origin of evil?

1. There cannot be thought without a thinker.
2. There is Thought in the universe.
3. Therefore there is a Thinker in the universe.
4. But a thinker is a Person.
5. Therefore there is a Personal Thinker in the universe.

You will grant me at least what Descartes made the basis of his philosophy, *Cogito, ergo sum:* "I think, therefore I am." I know that I think, and therefore I know that I am, and that I am a person. Agassiz says, in his Essay on Classification, that the universe "exhibits thought;" and that is not a very heterodox opinion. You know with what magnificent logical, rhetorical, and moral power, the massive Agassiz, in that best of his books, gathers up range after range of the operations of the natural laws, and closes every paragraph with this language: "These facts exhibit thought," "these facts exhibit mind;" and so on and on, across heights of intellectual scenery, gigantic as his own Alps, and as little likely to be pulverized. [Applause.] When that man, in presence of the scientific world, bowed his head in silent prayer in the face of the audience at Penikese, he did it before a Person. What cared he for the lonely few sciolists who assume that there is no reason for holding their heads otherwise than erect in this universe? As I contrast his mood and theirs, I think always of the old apologue of the heavy heads of wheat, and light heads: the heavy heads always bend. [Applause.]

You say that you are sure you are a thinker, because you know there is thought in you. *I know there is a Thinker in the universe, because there is Thought in it; and there cannot be thought without a thinker.* [Applause.] There cannot be a here without a there. There cannot be a before without an after. Just so, in the nature of things, there cannot be a Thought without a Thinker. If we know there is Thought in the universe, let us quit all doubt about a Divine Thinker.

What! falling into anthropomorphism, are you? That is a long word; but it means making God too much like man. Stern Ethan Allen, who made a speech once near Lake George, in a fort the ruins of which were part of my playground in earliest years, said, in a book written to attack Christianity, "There must be some resemblance between the divine nature and the human nature. I do know some things, and God knows all things; and therefore, in a few particulars, there is resemblance between man and God" (*Oracles of Reason*). Anthropomorphism, or the likening of God to man, is not quite as bad as likening God to mere blind physical force, is it? Most of those who are shyest of what is called anthropomorphism are advocates of a theory which likens God to what? To the highest we know? Not at all. To the next to the highest? No. They liken him to one of the lowest things we know,— to mere physical force, which has in itself no thought or will.

Force, the unknown God, forsooth? No doubt He whom we dare not name is behind all force; but to take one of the lower manifestations of his power as that according to which we will describe his whole nature is far more scandalous than to take the loftiest we know, and to say that God at least is equal to that; and how much better neither man nor angel knows, or ever will. [Applause.] Descartes wrote, in a passage closely following his famous aphorism, and which ought to be as famous as that: "I must have been brought into existence by a Being at least as perfect as myself." The Maker must be better than his work. "He must transcend in excellence my highest imagination of perfection."

Is it anthropomorphism to say that there cannot be thought without a thinker, and that there is Thought, and that therefore there must be a Thinker, in the universe? That is a necessary conclusion from self-evident, intuitive, axiomatic truth. It is an inference as tremorless as the assertion, that, if there is a *here*, there is a *there*. So are we made, that we cannot deny, that, if there is Thought in the universe, there must be a Thinker. Gentlemen, let us rejoice with a gladness as shoreless and reverent as this noon above our heads. Let us occupy our privileges. Let our souls go out to Him who holds the infinities and eternities in his palm as the small dust of the balance! Let our thoughts, if possible, not faint as they pass from the planet which He governs by his will called gravitation, or from the winkings of our eyelids, which the Asiatic proverb says are numbered, up to the star surf of the galaxies in which all the drops are known by name to Him who makes no mistake. This Thinker, with omnipotence and omniscience revealed by his works, ought to be holy. His unfathomable greatness raises the presumption of his holiness.

But we are not left in doubt upon this theme; for special light is given in the universe wherever doubt would be the most dangerous.

6. Every law in nature is the method of action of some will.

Having on previous occasions presented to you the proof of that proposition which ninety-five out of a hundred of the foremost names in physical science assert, I need do now no more than recite the names of Dana, Agassiz, Carpenter, Faraday, Helmholtz, Wundt, and Lotze, in support of a truth which transfigures the universe. (See closing chapters of CARPENTER'S *Mental Physiology*.)

7. There is in the universe an eternal law which makes for righteousness.

Matthew Arnold is authority for that, although his outlook on religious science and philosophy is much like a woman's outlook on politics. [Applause.]

8. The existence of that law is revealed in all outer experience or history.

Even Matthew Arnold says, that, if you wish to know that fire will burn, you can put your hand in it and obtain proof; and that you can, in the same experimental way, convince yourself that there is in history a Power, not ourselves, that makes for righteousness.

9. This law is revealed with vividness in the inner experience in all the natural operations of conscience.

10. There is, therefore, in the universe a Holy Will.

11. But a Holy Will can belong only to a Holy Person.

12. But we know that the moral law is perfect; for it requires invariably and unconditionally *what ought to be*.

A fathomless deep that word *ought!* An intuition of rightness and oughtness lies at the centre of it. In every individual, moral good is simply *what ought to be*, and moral evil *what ought not to be*, in the choices of the soul among motives.

13. The Maker must be more glorious than the thing made.

14. *The perfection of the moral law inhering in the nature of things proves the perfection of the Divine Nature.*

15. *The perfection of the moral law is a self-evident, axiomatic, intuitive truth.*

16. *All objections to the belief that God is perfect are, therefore, shattered upon the incontrovertible fact of the perfection of the moral law.*

17. The perfection of the Divine Nature having been proved on the basis of axiomatic truth, it follows that the present system of the universe is the best possible system, and that the present moral government of the world is the best possible moral government of the world.

18. *In all investigations concerning the origin of evil, we must keep in the foreground the axiomatically demonstrated fact of the perfection of the Divine Nature.*

Gentlemen, there is no one here deeply impressed with the duty of using intuition, instinct, syllogism, and experiment as tests of truth, who will not grant me the proposition that there is a perfect moral law in the universe. There is no man here who grants me that proposition, who can analyze it in the light of self-evident truth, and not find himself obliged to admit, that, as there is a perfect moral law, there must be a perfect moral lawgiver. You will allow me, in view of previous discussions here, to use, from this point onwards, the incontrovertible deliverance or the intuitional philosophy, *that the existence in the nature of things of a perfect moral law implies the existence in the universe of a holy will; which will can belong only to a Perfect Person.*

The perfection of the Divine Nature having been proved from the perfection of the moral law, what inferences follow as to the origin of evil?

1. It is a self-evident or intuitive truth that sin exists in this world.

2. God is perfect.

3. *Why did God permit sin to exist?*

4. *Of the many answers to this question, all are, perhaps, conjectures.*

Take up Kant, and read his discussion of "Religion inside the Range of Mere Reason," and you will find him concluding that the moral law itself, which he regarded as the sublimest thing known to man, cannot be quite explained to the human understanding. We know that this law has unconditioned authority; and yet, if we try to go behind its unconditional "categorical imperative," "Thou oughtest" and "Thou shalt," we find ourselves stopped by something beyond our comprehension, although not behind our apprehension. Just so Julius Müller, discussing the topic of the origin of evil, quotes this language of Kant's, and says that the student of religious science need not be ashamed to say that the origin of evil is involved in much mystery (MÜLLER, *Doctrine of Sin*, vol. ii. p. 172). Although we can know some things, we do not pretend to know all things, concerning it. We may make many conjectures concerning it; we may say that it arises in the abuse of the free will: but what led to that abuse of free will? The very arbitrariness of will when it chooses evil — was that the cause of the abuse of free will by itself? Müller, you will remember, teaches explicitly, as Kant did implicitly, that the origin of evil is to be referred back to an extra-temporal existence, where conditions unknown to man brought about the first sin. He would account for the origin of evil, not by what we see in this world, but by what may have occurred in some state of existence before this, and in which man was implicated as a personality. I am not adopting that portion of Julius Müller's scheme of thought. Many of the deepest students of the theme affirm that we cannot explain the origin of evil without going back to a state of existence previous to this.

5. Even among conjectures there may be a great choice.

6. Is sin permitted, as a dragooning process, to eventuate in good at last?

No: for then sin ought to be; and conscience affirms that it ought not to be.

Is sin the necessary means of the greatest good?

No; for the same reason.

Has all sin an ultimately beneficial effect? or is every fall a fall upward?

No; for, if this be the case, there is reason to doubt whether God is perfectly benevolent.

Let us suppose that there stands on the right, here in the universe, a marble staircase, and on the left a staircase of red-hot iron. Let both ascend to the same height, namely, to a universe from which all sin shall be eliminated. You go up by the marble staircase; you reach that stage,— a universe in which there is no sin. You go up by the red-hot iron staircase; you reach the same stage,— a universe in which there is no sin. I beg you to be cautious now and here lest you be misled. I warn you that just here is the place where you will think I was too rapid, and that you did not quite know what you admitted. You say that all penalty for sin has a remedial tendency, and that ultimately we shall reach a state in which there will be no evil in the universe. Men are going up the red-hot iron staircase. This represents the path of their suffering for sin. Ultimately, however, this staircase, you say, will bring all who go up it into freedom from all sin.

Be mercilessly clear. Could not God take men up the marble staircase to that same height? "Yes," you say. "He is omnipotent, omniscient." Do you admit that? Immense consequences turn on your being clear just here. God might take men up the marble staircase, which represents the path of holy free choice, and freedom from the penalties of sin. A universe free from sin is what you wish to reach. Men may be taken up this marble staircase to that height; or they may be taken up the red-hot iron staircase of suffering to the same height.

I affirm that your theory of evil is dishonorable to God; for we do know that men are going up on the fiery staircase. They are suffering remorse; they are filled with anguish; and the outcome of all that suffering is to be only the attaining of a height to which God, according to your theory, might have raised them without any suffering at all. *Therefore here are useless pains. He who inflicts them cannot be supremely benevolent.* You might attain the platform which represents the absence of sin from the universe by that marble staircase: you are attaining it by the red-hot iron staircase. Why does he permit men to ascend to that height by pain, when they might ascend to the same height without pain? *If he has no motive in that red-hot iron staircase, except to take men up, why does he not take men up by the cold marble?* He is not taking men up by the cold marble: he is taking them up the other way. But if, as you say, he has no motive but to take men up; if, as Theodore Parker said, every fall is a fall upward,

— how are you to prove the divine benevolence, face to face with his preference for that staircase, when he might have chosen the other?

Assuredly, the theory that all evil is a dragooning process, and that evil is the necessary means to the greatest good, not only is false to the intuitions which declare that evil ought not to be, but is in conflict with the truth that God is perfect. You cannot make it clear that God is perfect, if every fall is a fall upward; for men might go up the marble staircase, whereas they do go up by the red-hot iron. *There is some other reason for the red-hot iron than to take men up.*

The theory that every fall is a fall upward dishonórs God. I know not but that billions of times more spirits go up the marble staircase than up the red-hot staircase; but, if billions and billions do go that way, why could not you or I go that way.

It is inadmissible to assert that a benevolent Being chooses to subject his creatures to extreme pain, and attains by that means nothing that he might not attain without pain.

What answer does religious science give to the question as to the origin of evil? On this theme there are two strategic questions:

1. Can God prevent sin in a moral system?
2. Can God prevent sin in the best moral system?

Go to New Haven, and from the pupils of one of the profoundest and most original of New-England theologians, Dr. N. W. Taylor, you will find authority for answering these questions in this way:

1. "Can God prevent sin in a moral system?" —"We do not know that he can."

2. "Can God prevent sin in the best moral system?"—"No."—"How do you know?"—"Because he has not prevented it." [Applause.] (See TAYLOR's *Moral Government.*)

Go to Andover and ask these questions, and you will find them answered in this way:

1. "Can God prevent sin in a moral system?"— "Yes."—"How do you know?"—"Because he that can create can do any thing that is an object of power. God can do any thing that does not involve self-contradiction. We must suppose that a system of living beings, all with free wills, might be so influenced by motives as to retain their free will, and yet not sin. God can prevent sin in *a* moral system."

"Can God prevent sin in the *best* moral system?" —"No."—"How do you know?"—"Because he has not prevented it."

The Divine Perfection is proved by the perfection of the moral law. Sin exists. There is no conclusion possible, except that sin cannot be prevented wisely.

What are possibly some of the reasons why a perfect God cannot wisely prevent sin in the best moral system?

1. In the nature of things, there cannot be an upper without an under, a right without a left, a before without an after, a good without, at least, the possibility of evil.

2. *In the nature of things, the gift of free agency*

carries with it the possibility that the wrong as well as the right may be chosen.

3. In the nature of things, a created being must be a finite being.

4. In the nature of things, a finite is an imperfect being.

5. *In the nature of things, there will be the possibility of less than absolutely perfect action in every less than absolutely perfect agent.*

6. Man is such an agent.

Julius Müller and Tholuck, in their earlier years, were wont to fall into long conversations upon the origin of evil; and they at last fastened upon Leibnitz's great thought, that the necessary limitations of power and wisdom in all finite beings leave open a possibility to evil. Do not think Leibnitz asserted that the limitations of the finite creature make evil necessary. He asserts only that they make evil possible. I know that I am here not following the authority of Dr. Hodge of Princeton, who asserts that Leibnitz makes evil a necessity in the universe. He does not, if Julius Müller understands him. And, if some reading of the Theodicee proves any thing to me, Leibnitz means to assert only that the *possibility* of evil inheres in the very nature of things. If there is to be a created being brought into existence, that created being must be finite; and as such must be, to a certain extent, an imperfect being; and so *may,* not *must,* fall into sin. While the *possibility* of sin arises thus from the necessary limitation of the wisdom and power of created beings, the *fact* of sin, according to Leibnitz, comes from abuse of free will. (See Müller, *Doctrine of Sin*, vol. i., p. 276.)

7. It may be that God cannot prevent sin, if he deals with finite creatures according to what is due to himself.

8. It may be better to allow free agents to struggle with sin, and thus grow in the vigor of virtue, than to preserve them from such struggle, and thus allow them to remain weak.

But, my friends, let us rejoice, that, after proving the Divine Perfection, we know enough for our peace as to the origin of evil. It is not at all necessary to establish the soundness of any of these conjectures; for none of them are needed to prove that God is perfect.

In the heavens of the soul there ride unquenchable constellations, which assert that we alone are to blame if we do what conscience says we *ought* not to do. We are just as sure of the fact that we, and only we, are to blame when we do what conscience pronounces *wrong*, as we are of our own existence. Our demerit is a self-evident fact. All men take such guilt for granted. We know that we are responsible as surely as we all know that we have the power of choice. We know both facts from intuition. Our existence we know only by intuition; and by that same axiomatic evidence we know our freedom. How does sin originate in us? By a bad free choice. Just so it originated in the universe. But God brought us into existence. Yes; and he maintains us in existence. Very well; but the axioms of self-evident truth prove that he has given to us free will. The ocean floats the piratical vessels; the sea-breeze fills the sails of the pirate; but neither the ocean nor the sea-breeze is to blame for piracies. [Applause.]

VIII.

THE RELIGION REQUIRED BY THE NATURE OF THINGS.

THE SIXTY-SIXTH LECTURE IN THE BOSTON MONDAY LECTURESHIP, IN TREMONT TEMPLE FEB. 19.

"Um Mitternacht
 Kämpft ich die Slacht,
 O Menscheit, deiner Leiden:
 Nicht konnt ich sie entscheiden
 Mit meiner Macht
 Um Mitternacht.

 Um Mitternacht
 Hab' ich die Macht,
 Herr über Tod und Leben,
 In deine Hand gegeben:
 Du hältst die Wacht
 Um Mitternacht."
                    RÜCKERT.

"Miraris tu si Deus ille bonorum amantissimus, qui illos quam optimos esse atque excellentissimos vult, fortunam illis cum quâ exercentur adsignat?" — SENECA.

VIII.

THE RELIGION REQUIRED BY THE NATURE OF THINGS.

PRELUDE ON CURRENT EVENTS.

It would be a sad whim in the art of metallurgy if men should take up the notion that a white-heat is not useful in annealing metals; and so it is a sad whim in social science when men think that the white-heat we call a religious awakening is not useful in annealing society. Twice this nation has been annealed in the religious furnace just previously to being called on to perform majestic civil duties. You remember that the thirsty, seething, tumultuous, incalculably generative years from 1753 to 1783, or from the opening of the French war to the close of the Revolution, were preceded by what is known to history as the Great Awakening in New England in 1740, under Whitefield and Edwards. So, too, in 1857, when we were on the edge of our civil war, the whole land was moved religiously, and thus prepared to perform for itself and for mankind the sternest of all the political tasks that have been imposed in this century upon any civilized people.

But our short American story is no exception to the universal experiences of social annealing.

Discussing the subtler meaning of the Reformation, Carlyle says, "Once risen into this divine white-heat of temper, were it only for a season and not again, a nation is thenceforth considerable through all its remaining history. What immensities of *dross* and crypto-poisonous matter will it not burn out of itself in that high temperature in the course of a few years! Witness Cromwell and his Puritans, making England habitable even under the Charles Second terms for a couple of centuries more. Nations are benefited, I believe, for ages, by being thrown once into divine white-heat in this manner" (CARLYLE, *History of Frederick*, vol. i. book 3, chap. viii.).

That is the historial law for nations, for cities, for individuals. Do not be afraid of a white-heat: it is God's method of burning out dross. [Applause.]

Standing where Whitefield stood, on the banks of the Charles, a somewhat unlettered but celebrated evangelist, years ago, face to face with the culture of Harvard, was accused of leading audiences into excitement. "I have heard," said he in reply, "of a traveller who saw at the side of the way a woman weeping, and beating her breast. He ran to her and asked, 'What can I do for you? What is the cause of your anguish?'—'My child is in the well; my child is in the well!' With swiftest despatch assistance was given, and the child rescued. Farther on this same traveller met another woman wailing also, and beating her breast. He came swiftly to her, and with great earnestness asked, 'What is your trouble?'—'My pitcher is in the well; my pitcher is in the well!' Our great social and political excitements are all about pitchers in wells, and our religious excitements are about children in wells." [Applause.] A rude metaphor, you say, to be used face to face with Harvard; but a distinguished American professor, repeating that anecdote in Halle-on-the-Saale in Germany yonder, Julius Müller heard it and repeated it in his university; and it has been used among devout scholars all over Germany. Starting here on the banks of the Charles, and listened to, I presume, very haughtily by Cambridge and Boston, it has taken root in a deep portion of German literature as one of the classical illustrations of the value of a white-heat. [Applause.]

We must beware how we fall into pride at the size of our present religious audiences; for Boston has seen greater assemblies than are now gathered here in revivals. I hold in my hand a very significant portion of George Whitefield's journal, written in 1740 in this city. Let us not forget that the doctrine of the new birth, which was drawn so incisively on the mind of New England by Whitefield and Edwards that it seems commonplace now, was, in their time, and in the form in which they taught the truth, a disturbing novelty. The doctrine of the new birth as an acertainable change was not generally admitted in the religious portion of any New-England community when the awakening of 1740 began.

(See TRACY, *History of the Great Awakening*, pp. 46, 130.) Whitefield taught, to the dismay of New England, that a man does not become a saint in his sleep; and that credible evidence of personal entrance upon a life of love of what God loves, and of hate of what God hates, should be required before a man is made a member of the church; and that especially this change must take place in a minister; otherwise he is unfit to lead the living or the dead. These doctrines were not new to our Puritan fathers in 1640. But in 1740, under the political pressure caused by allowing only church-members to vote, and which led to the vastly mischievous, half-way covenant, by which persons not pretending to have entered on a new life at all were admitted to the church, we had lost the scientifically severe ideals of Plymouth Rock. It was a novel theory to us, that a man should be inexorably required to give credible evidence of a new life, as a condition of being allowed to preach.

"I insisted much on the doctrine of the new birth," writes Whitefield (*Journals in New England*, London, 1741, p. 48), "*and also on the necessity of a minister's being converted before he could preach aright. Unconverted ministers are the bane of the Christian church. I think that great and good man, Mr. Stoddard, is much to be blamed for endeavoring to prove that unconverted men might be admitted into the ministry.* A sermon lately published by Mr. Gilbert Tennent, entitled 'The Danger of an Unconverted Ministry,' I think unanswerable." "The 'spirit of the Lord enabled me to speak with such vigor against sending unconverted ministers into the ministry, that two ministers, with tears in their eyes, publicly confessed that they had lain hands on two young men, without so much as asking them whether they were born again of God or not" (p. 53).

Whitefield spoke with such vigor on this topic, that at this moment we need no speaking on it at all. Rhetorical students sometimes express amazement at the ineffectiveness of the printed addresses of Whitefield when read to-day; but they contain little that is new now, because they impressed so powerfully so much that was new then. Their present ineffectiveness arises from their past effectiveness.

"Mr. Edwards," Whitefield wrote at Northampton (this is Jonathan Edwards, of whom you may have heard) "is a solid and excellent Christian. I think I may say I have not seen his equal in all New England" (p. 45). "He is a son himself, and hath also a daughter of Abraham for his wife. A sweeter couple I have not yet seen. Their children were dressed not in silks and satins, but plain. She talked feelingly and solidly of the things of God. She caused me to renew those prayers which I have put up to God, that he would be pleased to send me a daughter of Abraham to be my wife. I find, upon many accounts, it is my duty to marry" (p. 46). "Minister and people wept much" (p. 46). "Dear Mr. Edwards wept during the whole time of exercise" (p. 47).

You say that in Boston yesterday, in audiences of six thousand and seven thousand, women wept too much, and that men were excited; but in 1740 men like Jonathan Edwards wept; and he is supposed to have had a head as well as a heart.

Gaze a moment on what this city of Boston did when she was hardly more than a village, and while the frontier settlements of New England were yet in danger of intrusions from the savages. All that was mortal of George Whitefield lies on the shore of the sea at Newburyport yonder, at rest until the heavens be no more. When he bade adieu to New England, he spoke on the Boston Common, the very soil over which every day you and I are walking lightly, and wondering whether we cannot go hence in peace, whatever we do. This orator writes in Boston, Sunday, Oct. 12, 1740, while no doubt the transfiguration of gold and russet and crimson hung upon some of the trees, of which we can now almost hear the whispering: "I went with the governor in his coach to the Common, where I preached my farewell sermon to nearly thirty thousand people, — a sight I have not seen since I left Blackheath, and a sight, perhaps, never before seen in America. It being duskish before I had done, the sight was more solemn. Numbers, great numbers, melted into tears when I talked of leaving them. I was very particular in my application, both to rulers, ministers, and people; commended what was commendable; blamed what was blameworthy; and exhorted my hearers steadily to imitate the piety of their forefathers; so that, whether I was present or whether I was absent, I might hear of their affairs, that with one heart and mind they were striving together for the faith of the gospel" (p. 53). So Boston responded to the memory of Cromwell and Hampden and Milton. She was young, and she yet is in the gristle. Is there better blood to put into her veins than that of our fathers? [Applause.]

THE LECTURE.

When Ulysses sailed past the isle of the sirens, who had the power of charming by their songs all who listened to them, he heard the sorcerous music on the shore; and, to prevent himself and his crew from landing, he filled their ears with wax, and bound himself to the mast with knotted thongs. Thus, according to the subtle Grecian story, he passed safely the fatal strand. But when Orpheus, in search of the Golden Fleece, went by this island, he, being, as you remember, a great musician, set up better music than that of the sirens, enchanted his crew with a melody superior to the alluring song of the sea-nymphs; and so, without needing to fill the Argonauts' ears with wax, or to bind himself to the mast with knotted thongs, he passed the sorcerous shore, not only safely, but with disdain.

The ancients, it is clear from this legend, understood the distinction between morality and religion. He who, sailing past the island of temptation, has enlightened selfishness enough not to land, although he rather wants to; he who, therefore, binds himself to the mast with knotted thongs, and fills the ears of his crew with wax; he who does this without hearing a better music, is the man of mere morality. Heaven forbid that I should underrate the value of this form of cold prudence; for wax is not useless in giddy ears, and Aristotle says youth is a perpetual intoxication. Face to face with sirens, thongs are good, though songs are better.

> "Sin hath long ears. Good is wax,
>   Wise at times the knotted thongs;
> But the shrewd no watch relax,
>   Yet they use like Orpheus songs.
> They no more the Sirens fear;
>   They a better music hear."

When a man of tempestuous, untrained spirit must swirl over amber and azure and purple seas, past the isle of the sirens, and knots himself to the mast of outwardly right conduct by the thongs of safe resolutions, although as yet duty is not his delight, he is near to virtue. He who spake as never mortal spoke saw such a young man once, and, looking on him, loved him, and yet said, as the nature of things says also, "One thing thou lackest." Evidently he to whom duty is not a delight does not possess the supreme prerequisite of peace. In presence of the siren shore, we can never be at rest while we rather wish to land, although we resolve not to do so. Only he who has heard a better music than that of the sirens, and who is affectionately glad to prefer the higher to the lower good, is, or in the nature of things *can* be, at peace. Morality is Ulysses bound to the mast. Religion is Orpheus listening to a better melody, and passing with disdain the sorcerous shore. [Applause.]

Aristotle was asked once what the decisive proof is that a man has acquired a good habit. His answer was, "The fact that the practice of the habit involves no self-denial of predominant force among the faculties." Assuredly that is keen; but Aristotle is rightly called the surgeon. Until we do love virtue so that the practice of it involves no self-denial of that sort, it is scientifically incontrovertible, that we cannot be at peace. In the very nature of things, while Ulysses wants to land, wax and thongs cannot give him rest. In the very nature of things, only a better music, only a more ravishing melody, can preserve Orpheus in peace. This truth may be stern and unwelcome; but the Greek mythology and the Greek philosophy which thus unite to affirm it are as luminous as the noon.

What is the distinction between morality and religion, and how can the latter be shown by the scientific method to be a necessity to the peace of the soul?

1. Conscience demands that what *ought to be* should be *chosen* by the will.

2. In relation to persons, what we *choose* we *love*.

3. Conscience reveals a Holy Person, the Author of the moral law.

4. Conscience, therefore, demands that rightness and oughtness in motives should not only be obeyed, but loved.

5. It demands that the Ineffable Holy Person revealed by the moral law should not only be obeyed, but loved.

6. This is an unalterable demand of an unalterable portion of our nature.

7. As personalities, therefore, we must keep company with this part of our nature, and with its demand, while we exist in this world and the next.

8. The love of God by man is, therefore, inflexibly required by the nature of things. Of all the commandments of exact science this is the first: Thou shalt *love* the Lord thy God with all thy mind and might and heart and strength.

9. Conscience draws an unalterable distinction between loyalty and disloyalty to the Ineffable Holy Person the moral law reveals, and between the obedience of slavishness and that of delight.

10. Only the latter is obedience to conscience.

11. But morality is the obedience of selfish slavishness.

That sounds harsh; but by it I mean only that a man of mere morality is Ulysses bound with thongs. He intelligently chooses not to land; but he wishes to do so. He loves what conscience declares ought not to be. His chief motive is selfishness acting under the spur of fear. In the nature of things, the fear of the Lord is the beginning of wisdom; but the end of wisdom is the perfect *love* that casteth out fear. [Applause.] You say that I have been appealing to fear. Very well, that is the beginning of wisdom, and I do not revere highly any love of God that has never known any fear of God. Show me that kind of love of God which has not felt what the fear of God is, and I will show you not principle, but sentiment, not religion, but religiosity. Of necessity, loyalty fears disloyalty. But loyalty is love for the Holy Person the moral law reveals; and such love conscience inexorably demands as what *ought* to be.

12. Religion, as contrasted with morality, is the obedience of affectionate gladness. It is the proud, rejoicing, unselfish, adoring love which conscience demands of man for the Ineffable Holy Person which conscience reveals.

13. As such, only religion, and not morality, can harmonize the soul with the nature of things.

So much may be clearly demonstrated by exact research.

Shakspeare says of two characters who conceived for each other a supreme affection as soon as they saw each other,

"At the first glance they have changed eyes."
Tempest, act i. sc. 2.

The Christian is a man who has changed eyes with God. In the unalterable nature of things, he who has not changed eyes with God cannot look into his face in peace.

What is that love which conscience says ought to be given by the soul to the Ineffable Holy Person which the moral law reveals? Is it a love for a fragment of that person's character, or for the whole? for a few, or for the whole list, of his perfect attributes?

14. In the nature of things, a delight in not only a part, but in all, of God's attributes, is necessary to peace in his presence.

15. *A religion consisting in the obedience of affectionate gladness, or a delight in all God's attributes, is therefore scientifically known to be a demand of the nature of things.*

It will not be to-morrow, or the day after, that these fifteen propositions will cease to be scientifically certain. Out of them multitudinous inferences flow, as Niagaras from the brink of God's palm. In a better age, philosophy will often pause to listen to these deluging certainties poured from the Infinite Heights of the nature of things. The roar and spray of them almost deafen and blind whoever stands where we do now: but they are there, although we are deaf; they are there, although we are blind.

Three inferences from these fifteen propositions are of supreme importance:

1. It is a sufficient condemnation of any scheme of religious thought to show that it presents for worship not all, but only a fragment, of the list of the divine attributes.

2. A religion that is true to the nature of things in theory will, of course, be found to work well in practice. The true in speculation is that which is harmonious with the nature of things. The fortunate in experience is that which is in harmony with the nature of things. The true in speculation, therefore, will turn out to be the fortunate in experience when applied to practice. If a scheme of thought does not work well in the long ranges of experience, if it will not bear translation into life age after age, that scheme of thought is sufficiently shown to be in collision with the nature of things.

3. By all the tests of intuition, instinct, experiment, and syllogism, religious science must endeavor to obtain the fullest view possible to man of the whole list of the divine attributes.

What scheme of religious thought will bear these three tests best?

Does such underrating of the significance of sin, as Theodore Parker's absolute religion is guilty of, work well in the long range of experience? *All religious teaching that in a wide and multiplex trial does not bear good fruits is presumably out of accord with the nature of things.* Does the doctrine that every fall is a fall upward bear good fruits? Does the assertion that sin is a necessary, and, for the most part, an inculpable stage in human progress, improve society? Does the proposition that character does *not* tend to a final permanence, bad as well as good, and good as well as bad, work well when translated into life age after age?

Gentlemen, let us make a distinction between false and true liberalism. Let us speak with proper respect of a learned, cultured Christian liberalism. Let us speak with proper disrespect of a lawless, limp, lavender liberalism. It has been the fault of the latter style of unscientific liberalism in every age, and it is especially the fault of Theodore Parker's theism, that it represents only a fragment of the divine attributes as the whole list.

The supreme question, then, my friends, if you are convinced that man cannot have peace unless he has a delight in all attributes of the Holy Person revealed by the moral law, is to know what the full list is. Whether Boston cares, or Harvard, to know what the natural conditions of the soul's peace with the nature of things are, I do not know; but, for one, I feel very sure I am going hence, and that I wish to go hence in peace, and that I cannot go hence in peace unless I love, not only a fragment, but the whole list, of the divine attributes.

What can science of the ethical sort do toward presenting us with a full view of the divine attributes? That is a very central and a very strategic question. Suppose, in order to make our thoughts clear, that we begin our answer by substituting scientific for biblical phraseology. Try for once the experiment, and see how we shall come out. Everybody admits there is a nature of things. Now, what if we assert simply that it is necessary to the soul's peace to acquire harmony with the nature of things? Say nothing about God now. It is certain that there is in the universe what science calls the nature of things; and it is tolerably clear that that has not changed much for some years. [Applause.] It is without any variableness or shadow of turning. It was; it is; it is to come. For one, when I ask the question whether I can know God, I am always asking, immediately after that, whether I can know the nature of things. What if the nature of things is but another name for his nature? What if the nature of things, which has not changed in eternity past, and is not to change in eternity to come, is but a revelation of Him, with whom is no variableness, neither shadow of turning? I know that the nature of things is infinitely kind toward virtue. I know that the nature of things is infinitely stern toward vice. What if, while science gazes on the nature of things, and looks fixedly into it, she finds behind it the will of a personal God, omniscient, omnipotent, omnipresent, invisible, but in conscience spiritually tangible?

1. In the nature of things, to work for good is to work against evil.

Does anybody doubt this? Is not that a proposition just as clearly true as that a straight line is the shortest distance between two points, or that a thing cannot be, and not be, at the same time, and in the same sense, as any other intuitive deliverance of our faculties?

2. In the nature of things, God cannot work for good without working against evil.

I am assuming only that God cannot deny himself. That *cannot* is to me at once the most terrible and the most alluring certainty in the universe. He cannot deny the demands of his own perfections. These are another name for the nature of things. We feel sure, that, in the nature of things, there cannot be a here without a there, an upper without an under, or any working of God for good without working by him against evil. The nature of things is not fate, but the unchangeable free choice of infinite perfection in God.

Allow no one to mislead you by overlooking the distinctions between *certainty* and *necessity*, *will* and *shall*, *occasioning* and *necessitating*, *infallibly* certain and *inevitably* certain. Let no one assert that faithfulness to self-evident truths as to the nature of things leads to a system of thought consisting of adamantine fatalism. There can be but one best way in which to conduct the universe. Omniscience will know that way. Omnipotence will choose and adhere to that way. There will be no deviation from that way in the course of the government of the universe. There will thus appear to be fate in the infinities and eternities; but there is there in reality only the infinitely wise and holy, and therefore unchanging, free choice of Almighty God.

Even man's free will may illustrate the law of *certainty* without falling at all under that of *necessity*.

Near the great sea there lives yonder at Salisbury a renowned poet, on whom the light of the golden Indian summer of genius is now shining. It was once my surprising fortune to hear this revered man say seriously that he could not quite agree with Andover and Jonathan Edwards in wholly denying the freedom of the will. I made no attempt to correct this error; for I had proper reverence for that poet whom Germany regards as the deepest heart among all American writers of lyrics (see BROCKHAUS' *Conversations Lexicon*, art. " Whittier "), a man in whom there is an unquenchable Hebrew fire, which quite as effectively as any other flame, moved before us as a pillar of radiance in the dark days of our antislavery contest. [Applause.]

Now, it may be that Andover does not understand Jonathan Edwards; but she does not understand him to deny the freedom of the will. And as for denying the freedom of the will herself, you might as well ask whether Andover denies the immortality of the soul, or whether Jefferson Davis asserted that federal power ought to be supreme over State rights, or whether Plymouth Rock will float. There is no monstrosity greater as a misconception than to affirm that New-England theology denies the freedom of the will; and yet I see that affirmation made almost monthly by irresponsible scribblers, and now and then responsibly, over names which I honor.

3. In the nature of things, God is not God, unless he works for good.

4. Therefore, in the nature of things, he is not God, unless he works against evil.

5. He is perfect; and therefore, with all his attributes, he works for good.

6. He is perfect; and therefore, with all his attributes, he works against evil.

7. Sin exists in the universe by the abuse of free will.

It is incontrovertible that conscience declares that we, and we alone, are to blame when we do what we know to be wrong. Of course, I keep in mind the distinction between an error and sin, or between a mistake of the moral kind and a wrong of the moral kind. When I speak of sin, I mean a free choice of motives which conscience pronounces to be bad. In every bad free choice there comes upon the soul, after the act, a sense of personal demerit. If that deliverance of the self-evident truths of the soul is *not* to be received, several rather large results follow.

If you deny the intuition which proves that the will is free, you cannot prove your own existence; for you know your own existence only by intuition. How do I know there is an eternal world? By intuition. How do I know that I am in existence? By intuition. How do I know that I am personally to blame when I do what conscience pronounces wrong? By intuition. We are not to play fast and loose with this supreme test of truth. Intuition is the soul's direct vision of all truths which to man have these three characteristics, — *self-evidence, necessity, universality. An intuition may mean a truth, self-evident, necessary, and universal; or it may mean the act of the mind in beholding such a truth.* When I say any thing is affirmed by intuition, I mean that it is guaranteed by that capacity of the soul through which we have a direct vision of self-evident, axiomatic, necessary truth. It is an intuitive truth that the will is free; and, as Johnson used to say, "there is the end of it." We know we are to blame when we choose the wrong; and there is an end of that. If you know by self-evident, axiomatic, necessary, universal truth that you exist, you know by the same evidence that you are free, and that you have incurred personal demerit whenever you choose a motive which conscience pronounces to be a bad one.

What you take for granted in business, and in law, and in literature, you must allow me to take as proved in religious science.

Does anybody doubt that he is free in business? Very well: will anybody doubt, then, that he is free in religion? Does anybody doubt that God gives the harvest, but that nevertheless man must sow and plant? Does not the husbandman every spring go forth and act as if every thing depended on him? and does not God work with him to fill the valley with fatness? Just so in the spiritual realm: a man must go forth and sow good seed; and God will give the increase. There is no collision in business between freedom of will and fate; and so, as the laws of the universe are the same in both fields, there is no collision in religion. *Predestination* does not mean *destiny*. This is one of the most mischievous words in theology; and the trouble is with the syllable "dest." I never use the word predestination; for that syllable "*dest*" implies destiny, and destiny implies necessity. In religious science the word "predestination" does not mean necessity, but only certainty.

8. *While sin continues, God cannot forgive it without making the sinner worse.*

In this city six thousand people were told, the other evening, with great depth of thought, that if a child deliberately lies, and you forgive the child before he has exhibited any sorrow for the act, you make the child worse. That is, indeed, a very simple instance of the moral law; but in scientific minds there is no doubt that the moral law is equally universal with the physical. If you will measure a little arc of the physical law, you can measure the whole circle.

If I were to take flight into space, I should not run beyond the knowledge that I have acquired here of the law of gravitation. That law is one in all worlds so far as science knows. So, too, if I understand the properties of light here, I understand them in Orion and the Pleiades. A good terrestrial textbook on light or gravitation would be of service in the North Star. The universality and the unity of law make our earth, although but an atom, immensity itself in its revelations of truth. (See DANA, *Geology*, chap. 1.) Now, if I know that a man has deliberately lied to me, I cannot here, under the moral law, forgive him before he repents, without making him worse. If I know that, then there is reason to believe that God cannot, in the nature of things, forgive a free agent that has incurred personal demerit by the choice of wrong motives, till he has repented, without making that agent worse. [Applause.] The nature of things, gentlemen — it is the same yesterday, to-day, and forever.

Here is a Boston sonnet, entitled "A Far Shore;" and it asserts the universality of the moral law as well as of the physical and the organic; and so it applies not only to Greece and Italy, and the shadow of the Pyramids, but also to the shore of that undiscovered country from whose bourn no traveller returns:

> On a far shore my land swam far from sight,
>   But I could see familiar native stars;
>   My home was shut from me by ocean bars,
> Yet home hung there above me in the night;

THE RELIGION OF THE NATURE OF THINGS. 213

>Unchanged fell down on me Orion's light;
>>As always, Venus rose, and fiery Mars;
>>My own the Pleiads yet; and without jars
>In wonted tones sang all the heavenly height.
>So when in death, from underneath my feet
>>Rolls the round world, I then shall see the sky
>>Of God's truths burning yet familiarly;
>My native constellations I shall greet:
>>I lose the outer, not the inner eye,
>>The landscape, not the soul's stars, when I die.

[Applause.]

9. The self-propagating power of habit, acting in the sphere of holy affections, places the nature of things on the side of righteousness.

10. The same self-propagating power of habit, acting in the sphere of evil affections, arranges the nature of things against evil.

11. Good has but one enemy, the evil; but the evil has two enemies, the good and itself. [Applause.] (See JULIUS MÜLLER, *Doctrine of Sin*, vol. ii.)

12. Judicial blindness increases the self-propagating power of evil; remunerative vision increases the self-propagating power of holiness.

"Every man," says the Spanish proverb, "is the son of his own deeds." "Every action," says Richter, "becomes more certainly an eternal mother than it is an eternal daughter" (TITAN, vol. i. cycle 105). These are the irreversible laws according to which all character tends to a final permanence, good or bad.

13. God cannot give the wicked two chances without subjecting the good to two risks.

14. Self-evident truth shows that man is free.

15. Self-evident truth proves that man may attain a final permanence of character, good or bad, and in that state, not lose freedom of will.

16. *This may occur in the best possible universe, in which all things will of course work together for good to the good, and therefore, of necessity, for evil to the evil.*

Adhere to the proposition that there cannot be an upper without an under. *Can* God arrange the universe so that all things in it shall work together for the good of the good, without arranging it so that all things shall work together for the evil of the evil? *Can* God be God, and not arrange the universe so that all things in it shall work together for the good of the good? *Can* God be God, and not so arrange the universe, that all things shall work together for the evil of the evil? Follow the deliverance of your intuitional philosophy, that the soul is free. I know how a man is tempted here, and how a silly sciolism will overturn the testimony of the intuitions themselves, rather than admit that man is responsible for all action that conscience pronounces wrong. But, if you overturn the deliverance of the intuitions there, please overturn it elsewhere. You will not play fast and loose much longer, gentlemen; for our age is coming to be, thank God, unwilling to take any thing for granted, and more and more loyal to clear ideas. [Applause.] Our greatest philosophies, metaphysical and physical, all stand on the basis of self-evident truths, or intuition; and although your physicist who never has studied metaphysics does not know who sharpened his tools, or sometimes what his tools are, he every day is using self-evident truth, and stands on the intuitions at which he scoffs. You say that the intuitional philosophy sails by dead-reckoning. Well, dead-reckoning by axioms is scientific. You say that the philosophy of self-evident truths is off soundings, and that you prefer to keep in water where you can feel the bottom. I tell you that your sounding-lines themselves are spun by what you call dead-reckoning, or the philosophy of self-evident, axiomatic, necessary truths. [Applause.] Your physicist has no scientific rule, the validity of which is not guaranteed by self-evident truth; and so when you say I sail by dead-reckoning, and am off soundings, and that you are sounding and sounding, and that you know there is an external world, and that you believe only what you can see and touch and handle, I go behind your sounding-line, and ask, "Who spun that?" I ask, "How are you certain there is any external world?" You say, "It is evident." So I say, "It is self-evident." [Applause.] On self-evidence you stand, and on self-evidence I stand; and, if you and I can shake hands at this point, we shall never part. [Applause.] If we are true to the deliverance of all the intuitions, and not merely to a portion of them, we shall vividly behold truth of which neither materialism nor pantheism dreams. We shall see God in not merely a few of his attributes, but in that whole range of them, which the nature of things exposes to human vision; and we shall find it a thing just as glorious to be reconciled with God as it is to be reconciled with the nature of things, and just as little likely to occur in a man asleep, or by accident and haphazard, and dreaming and poetizing.

We shall find it a thing at least as terrible to fall under the power of God as it is to fall under the power of the nature of things. Assuredly the nature of things will not break the bruised reed, nor quench the smoking flax, of loyalty to itself; the nature of things assuredly, too, may be a consuming fire to all disloyalty to itself. [Applause.] It may be an omnipresent kiss or an omnipresent flame. The savages in Peru used to kiss the air as their profoundest sign of adoration to the collective divinities. The nature of things is above and around and beneath us; and our sign of adoration to it must be not slavish self-surrender, but affectionate, glad preference of what this unbending perfection requires.

You say the permanent existence of sin would be an impeachment of the divine benevolence. Why is not the beginning of it an impeachment? The mystery, my friends, is not, that, under the law of judicial blindness and the self-propagating power of habit, sin may continue: the mystery is, that sin ever was allowed to begin. *It has begun.* There is no doubt on that subject, and, when you will explain to me the consistency of your philosophy with the beginning of sin, I will explain to you the consistency of a final permanence of free evil character with that same philosophy. [Applause.]

What we do know is, that, the more a man sins

against light, the less sensitive he is to it. What we do know is, that over against judicial blindness stands remunerative vision, and we cannot change one law without changing the other. The nature of things is the flame; the nature of things is the kiss: God is God by being both. [Applause.] What God does is successfully done. What God does is well done.

Mrs. Browning, whom England loves to call Shakspeare's daughter, and who is in many respects the deepest interpreter of the modern cultivated heart and head, rests in God's goodness.

"Oh the little birds sang east, the little birds sang west!
And I said in underbreath, All our life is mixed with death,
And who knoweth which is best?

Oh the little birds sang east, the little birds sang west!
And I smiled to think God's goodness flows around our incompleteness;
Round our restlessness his rest."

Had she paused there, she would not have been the prophetess of science as she is; for, without resting in an unscientific liberalism, she says also:

" Let star-wheels and angel-wings, with their holy winnowings,
Keep beside you all your way,
Lest in passion you should dash, with a blind and heavy crash,
Up against the thick-bossed shield of God's judgment in the field."

Rime of the Duchess May.

[Applause.]

IX.

THEODORE PARKER ON COMMUNION WITH GOD AS PERSONAL.

THE SIXTY-SEVENTH LECTURE IN THE BOSTON MONDAY LECTURESHIP, IN TREMONT TEMPLE FEB. 26.

"Religion ist anfangs Gottlehre; recht ist sie Gottseligkeit. Auf Marktplatz und Schlachtfeld steh' ich mit zugeschlossener Brust, worin der Allhöchste und Allheiligste mit mir spricht, und vor mir als nahe Sonne ruht." — RICHTER: *Levana*.

"So schaff' ich am sausenden
Webstuhl der Zeit."
GOETHE: *Faust*.

IX.

THEODORE PARKER ON COMMUNION WITH GOD AS PERSONAL.

PRELUDE ON CURRENT EVENTS.

ONE day in Parliament William Pitt said, " I have no fear for England : she will stand till the day of judgment." But Edmund Burke replied, " What I fear is the day of *no* judgment." The relation of the temperance reform to the future of great cities has an unsounded depth of interest from Edmund Burke's point of view. In 1800 one twenty-fifth of the population of the United States was in towns numbering eight thousand or more inhabitants; in 1870 one-fifth (WALKER, *Statistical Atlas*, 1876).

Of course I need not emphasize the fact that many of our churches are doing their duty on the topic of temperance in great towns. I do not overlook starry exceptions. I remember that Roswell Hitchcock's church in New York was once called together in order that two persons who had joined it might have work assigned them on the church philanthropic committees. There was no other business before the gathering than to set two persons at work; the only ones out of a very large church who had not something definite to do in our sorely-tried metropolis. Other individual churches are active, but the mass of our churches are singularly inefficient [applause], in moral reform in cities. The other day I saw a heap of manuscript books, in which the names of the most abandoned streets and lanes in this city were written down, and in which a competent number of fit persons were assigned to the work of visitation in these desolate quarters. Now, is it not a circumstance rather humiliating that a man who is comparatively a stranger in this city must come half way across the continent to set us here in Boston at work which we ought to know better than he does how to do? Is it not a fact somewhat inexpressible in its wincing outcome, as it touches our poor pride, to know that many a town in New England, Boston not excepted from the list, is allowing a Young Men's Christian Association, for instance, that wishes to do just such work as this, to starve? You are not giving half money enough to the agents you employ for religious effort among the poor and degraded in cities; and you do not work yourselves. You act through the finger-tips of a few saints; women missionaries, city missionaries; and you are starving them. There is not a city missionary, there is not an established religious agency of yours among the perishing and dangerous classes and their fleecers, that has adequate financial support, to say nothing of sympathy. You say this is plain speech; but I had rather speak plainly than bring upon myself the charge of being inattentive to what has been brought so prominently before New England in the great audiences in the noon yonder in the Tabernacle, when reformed men have spoken and been addressed, in the presence of thousands, in tears. We need every season just such effort as is now making temporarily here for the abandoned quarters in this and other cities.

There is in Boston a great orator, whose name is a power from the surf of the Bay of Fundy to the waterfalls of the Yosemite. Stand in front of his house, in the street where Slavery once mobbed him, and you may count thirty grog-shops within sight of his windows. Yes: Wendell Phillips told you the other day that he could count thirty-nine, and that for thirteen of these only is Massachusetts law responsible. The truth is, that the Church, after all, is, or should be, the sheet-anchor of all moral reform. I do not undervalue Washingtonianism; I do not undervalue temperance legislation; in fact, although there may be no one prohibitory law with all the details of which I should sympathize, yet I must call myself a prohibitionist. [Cheers and a few hisses. Mr. Cook turned to the quarter from which the hisses proceeded, and said], Wait two hundred years, and see whether you will hiss prohibition! Wait until Macaulay's two hundred are the average number of inhabitants for every square mile between Plymouth Rock and the Golden Gate, and see whether you will hiss prohibition! Wait until a quarter of our population shall be massed in cities, and Edmund Burke's day of no judgment appears, and see whether you will hiss prohibition!

Massachusetts now has laws by which sales of liquor are forbidden at all times to minors and drunkards and to persons to whom the sellers have been requested to cease selling by their families or employers. Are you executing that law? The letting of real estate for the illicit selling of liquor is made more perilous by a new clause requiring the magistrate to serve notice of the conviction of any party of such an offence on the lessor of the premises. The latter is thereupon required, by the old law of common nuisance, to eject the tenant, under penalty. Are church-members in Massachusetts who own real estate in degraded quarters never implicated in the violation of that righteous public law?

America wants her churches to organize themselves for permanent and aggressive, just as they occasionally have organized themselves for temporary and timid, work for the squalid and debased. I read in the newspapers the other day that some noble women, lineal descendants, no doubt, of those whom Paul saw on Mars Hill, or of those who were among the most efficient of all the powers that cowed old Rome by the purity of Christian life, have gone into the jaws and throat of despair in certain abandoned quarters of this city, and have found homes for degraded women, and taken the almost incredible word of hope to persons like some to whom our Lord himself spoke. This work is going on silently; it must not be heralded. What is needed is that it should be made permanent. [Applause.]

Lessing said, that by and by, when the world has found out what church does the most good, it will know in what church to believe. [Applause.] Show me the church that is willing to wash the feet of the degraded; show me the church that goes about from house to house doing good; show me the church organized for permanent, aggressive, audacious, moral effort; show me a church that has not lost her Master's whip of small cords, and I will show you the church, and the only church, that can save America when she has two hundred inhabitants to the square mile. [Applause.]

There was in our Christian and Sanitary Commission in the civil war a great hint for our years of peace. The Sanitary Commission and the Christian Commission followed our armies like white angels; and why should not the flight of these two ministering spirits be in some sense perpetuated in our great cities, which are always battle-fields? One thousand years ago the Norsemen came up Boston Harbor in shallops, every one of which had on its sail a painting of a cormorant raven, and at its prow a wolf's head. Bryant says the Norse pirates sailed up yonder azure bay a thousand years ago. What I know is, that the Norse raven yet flies in America, and the Norse wolf yet howls. What I want to fly side by side with the raven, what I want to run side by side with the wolf, is organized, permanent, aggressive, audacious, deadly Christian effort. [Applause.]

New England has seen lately some new indications that temperance discussion in the church will be heard by the masses outside of it. Look at the Merrimack River and its cities, and notice what one man, Dr. Reynolds, has done there. You do not believe in all his methods, although experience is indorsing them significantly? Very well: will you invent better 'ones? [Applause.] What are we about, when men, and some women, through the country, more rapidly than under the scythe of war, are falling into their graves under the flame of these gross, consuming habits, that we do not turn all the moral power of the church, at least once a month in cities, on this conflagration? We have power to put down by moral suasion a great amount of this evil, and our responsibility is proportionate to our power. Let moral suasion once have free course, and legal suasion will follow of the right sort. Whenever temperance has tried to fly on one wing, that is, either with legal suasion alone on the one hand, or with moral suasion alone on the other, her flight has been a sorry spiral. She never will ascend to God, or even make the circuit of the globe, until she strikes the air with majestic equal vans keeping rhythm with each other, moral suasion and legal suasion, acting side by side, to bear her on, and to winnow the earth of both the tempters and the temptable.

Shrewd men ought to perceive that undefiled religion in the heart is the only adequate dissuasive from Circe's cup at the lips. "To conquer," said Napoleon, "we must replace." To conquer unholy passion we must replace it by holy passion. Undoubtedly a man may lose in the religious renovation of his nature his appetite for strong drink. It is, you say, a very vexed question, whether a converted man loses his appetite for liquor. Cases of deep inherited disease may be set aside as not under discussion here. Put this question on another plane of thought. Have you not known some men morally transfigured by the power of a supreme earthly affection? Have you not seen some father bereaved of a darling boy, and changed thereafter to the finger-tips? Have you not known often a great crisis in life to take a bad appetite out of a man, even when the crisis was merely secular? There are some derangements infinitely more infamous than inherited appetites for strong drink; but even these are often removed wholly by a holy love, filial, conjugal, or paternal, if once the affection takes hold of the deepest inmost in the soul. Can you not believe, that, when God is loved supremely, there may come to a man such an awakening of the upper zones of his nature, that he shall no longer have an appetite for strong drink? He, and only he, will be lifted above temptation who falls in love with God with all his heart.

THE LECTURE.

The Russian poet Derzhavin has the honor of having written an ode, to the rhythm of which all cultivated circles have bowed down, from the Yellow Sea westward to the Pacific. The stanzas of it you may see to-day embroidered on silk in the palaces of the Emperors of Japan and China. You will find the poem translated into Persian, into Arabic, into Greek, into Italian, into German; and, when I open the most popular of our American anthologies, I find that the book closes with this Russian anthem:

> "O Thou Eternal One, whose presence bright
> All space doth occupy, all motion guide,
> Unchanged through Time's all-devastating flight!
> Thou only God; there is no God beside!
> Being above all beings! Mighty One
> Whom none can comprehend and none explore,
> Who fill'st existence with thyself alone,
> Embracing all, supporting, ruling o'er,
> Being whom we call God, and know no more!
> . . . .
> God! thus alone my lowly thoughts can soar,
> Midst thy vast works admire, obey, adore;
> And when the tongue is eloquent no more,
> The soul shall speak in tears in of gratitude."
>
> *Translation of Sir John Bowring.*

When a poem has the majestic fortune to be adopted as a household word of culture in twenty nations, we are scientifically justified in the conclusion that the deep instincts of the human heart from the rising to the setting sun assert what the poem expresses. Thus we judge in the case of the songs of love; and so, I insist, we must judge in relation to the anthems of religion. Indeed, these latter sink more penetratingly into history than the former. Nothing is treasured by the best part of the world so painstakingly, from the epic we call the Book of Job to Derzhavin's poem on the Divine Nature, as the literature that is struck worthily to the keynote of adoration of the Infinite Perfection of a Personal God. This is a literary fact which the Matthew Arnolds and Herbert Spencers would do well to fathom. The native human instincts are ascertainable by the reception all races and tribes and tongues give to the literature of communion with God as personal. *Such instincts are a scientific proof of the existence of their correlate.* There can be no thought without a thinker. There is thought in the universe; therefore, there is a thinker in the universe. But a thinker is a person: therefore there is a Personal Thinker in the universe. There can be no such organic hungering as all nations have for communion with God as personal without the possibility of such communion. Men who revere the natural will not scorn Theism, for it is as natural as any thing else in nature. The veracity of our theistic instincts is proved by their naturalness. Julius Müller gives as one definition of religion the communion of the soul with God as personal.

1. Men as they are can be made holy only by loving a holy person.

2. Nothing so effectually purifies the heart as love; for nothing so effectually wooes us from selfishness.

3. There can be no love without trust, and no trust without purity.

4. Love produces in the lover the mood of the object loved.

5. Souls grow more by contact with souls than by all other means.

6. Growth, strength, bliss, arise naturally from spiritual love.

7. All these laws of the higher affections apply to the communion of the human spirit with the Ineffable Holy Person whom the moral law reveals.

8. Under these irreversible natural laws, religion is affectionate communion with God as personal.

In Locksley Hall, Tennyson, speaking merely as an observer of human nature in its social zone, utters one of the profoundest of all the truths of its religious zone, when he says,

" Love took up the harp of life; smote on all the chords with might;
Smote the chord of self, which, trembling, passed in music out of sight."

Is there any hand but that of love that can produce this effect? *Under natural law can man be made unselfish or holy in any other way than by loving a holy person?* Tennyson knows of no other way; religious science knows of no other.

The truth is, my friends, we are acquainted with no furnace which will burn selfishness out of a man, except this fiery bliss we call a supreme spiritual affection. There is admiration of men by each other; but there is no burning the selfishness out of men until they come to trust and to love, and to that interspheríng of soul by soul which is always the result of trust of the transfigured sort, — one of the rarest things on earth. Do not think that I am putting before you a low ideal of trust; for I speak of those forms of love — conjugal, filial, paternal — which the poets love to glorify.

I read the other day two Boston sonnets entitled "Trust," which made of the crystalline window of one of the deepest human experiences an opening through which to look into the sky behind the sky.

> I know that thou art true and strong and pure.
>   My forehead on thy palm, I fall asleep:
>   My sentinels with thee no vigils keep,
> Though elsewhere never without watch secure.
> How restful is thy palm! I life endure:
>   These stranger souls whose veils I shyly sweep,
>   These doubts what secrets hide within the deep,
> Because, aglow within the vast obscure,
>   Thy hand is whitest light! My peace art thou;
>   My firm green isle within a troubled sea;
>   And, lying here, and looking upward now,
> I ask, if thou art this, what God must be:
>   If thus I rest within thy goodness, how
>   In goodness of the infinite degree?

But there are lightnings wherever there is love; for character cannot have one side without having two sides; we cannot love good, and not abhor evil; and so the second sonnet, equally true to trust, contrasts with the first:

> This crystal soul of thine, were it outspread
>   Until the drop should fill the universe,
>   How in it might the angels' wings immerse;
> And wake and sleep the living and the dead;
> Bereaved eyes bathe; rest Doubt its tossing head;
>   Swim the vast worlds; dissolve Guilt's icy curse;
>   And sightless, if but loyal, each disperse
> Fear by full trust, and, by devotion, dread!
>   And yet these perfect eyes in which mine sleep
>   Would not be sweet were not their lightning deep.

In softest skies the swiftest fire-bolts dwell.
Thine eyes mix dew and flame, and both are well.
If thus I fear this soul, O God! how thee,
Both love's and lightning's full infinity?
[Applause.]

In the Portuguese Sonnets, the most subtle and tender and sublime expressions of affection ever written by woman, it is not so much Mrs. Browning who sings, as Robert Browning, the future husband. When Tennyson, in the In Memoriam commemorates the young Hallam, it is not Tennyson who sings, so much as Hallam. When Robert Hall and Canning form a friendship for each other at Eton, it is Canning who appears in Hall, and Hall who appears in Canning. When Thomas Carlyle, John Sterling, and Edward Irving, are friends, it is Irving that appears in Carlyle at times, and Carlyle that appears in Irving; and, when Sterling lies dying, it is Carlyle that makes up more than half his soul. Always when two human personalities are united by a supreme spiritual affection, they intersphere each other, and produce the moods of one in the other; and, when there is a transfiguration in personal affection, there is thus a smiting of the chord of self, till it passes in music out of sight. Of course, therefore, there is no method to produce growth, strength, and bliss in the soul, like the pure contact of spirit with spirit. Carlyle says we grow more by contact of soul with soul than by all other means united. Literature, if possessed of power, is the mirror of soul, and causes those who love it to grow by contact with the pulsating, reflected depths of genius.

But a Persian proverb says, "Look into the sky to find the moon, and not into the pool." Look into the faces of your elect living friends, and into the souls of those whom you trust most. Make much of your giant friendships of all kinds, and be thankful if you have one genuine friendship of any kind, and let unforced trust enswathe you, if you would be transfigured. You grow more in these high moments of personal affection when you look at the moon in the sky than by much meditating on the moon in the pool. Friendships with authors and heroes in a far past are undoubtedly honorable to us, and transfiguring, and in loneliness are, perhaps, the highest human solace; but they are not the highest possible to man; they are not the moon in the sky.

Gentlemen, you all foresee that I am to affirm that a human spirit may commune with the Infinite Spirit, and that all these laws of transfiguration are to be kept in view when we would explain the renovating power on man of the communion of the soul with God as personal. You anticipate that in a moment I shall be asking, in the name of the scientific method, that you, face to face with the Holy Person the conscience reveals, should give free course to all those majestic natural laws by which soul transfigures soul through personal affection. Gentlemen, I do ask this, and in the stern name of the scientific method. Is any one thinking, that, as a benighted soul, brought up in the mossy mediævalism of our latest theology, I cannot worship one

God, because I believe in three Gods? Do not pity mediævalism too much; it knows the difference between Trinity and Tritheism. I wish just now to thank God, if you can worship one God as Derzhavin does. I rejoice with you, if you can go as far as scientific Theism does, and worship one God, who was, who is, who is to come. Let us to-day not go farther than with Derzhavin to admire, obey, adore One King, eternal, immortal, invisible, and in conscience spiritually tangible.

Samuel Johnson, when he had finished his great dictionary, received a note from his publisher in these words: "Andrew Miller sends his compliments to Samuel Johnson, with the money in payment for the last sheet of his dictionary, and thanks God he is done with him." To this rude note Johnson replied, "Samuel Johnson sends his compliments to Andrew Miller, and is very glad to notice, as he does by his note, that Andrew Miller has the grace to thank God for any thing." [Applause.] You call yourselves deists; you call yourselves theists; you hold, that, in the name of science, we can worship one God, who must be behind all natural law. I thank God that you believe as much as that. Perhaps more lies wrapped up and capsulate in your belief than you think. Here are a few slight notes from a Boston marching-song, on which my eyes fell the other day, when I was alone. They are sung in the name of exact science; and surely we can sing together any thing attuned to that key-note.

Bounds of sun-groups none can see;
Worlds God droppeth on his knee;
Galaxies that loftiest swarm,
Float before a loftier Form.

Mighty the speed of suns and worlds;
Mightier who these onward hurls;
Pure the conscience's fiery bath;
Purer fire God's lightning hath.

Brighter He who maketh bright
Jasper, beryl, chrysolite;
Lucent more than they whose hands
Girded up Orion's bands.

Sweet the spring, but sweeter still
He who doth its censers fill;
Good is love, but better who
Giveth love its power to woo.

Lo, the Maker! greater He,
Better, than His works must be:
Of the works the lowest stair
Thought can scale, but fainteth there.

Thee with all our strength and heart,
God, we love for what Thou art;
Ravished we, obedient now,
Only, only perfect Thou!

[Applause.]

Will you sing that tremorless song of science, and keep entranced, stalwart step to your singing, and then turn to me and say that these sublime natural principles by which human affection transfigures the soul do not apply in the sphere of man's relations to the Ineffable Holy Person the moral law reveals? There is such a law; there is such a person. It follows that there are relations between that holy person and ourselves. In the name of ascertained natural law, I affirm that men as they are can be made holy only by loving a holy person. [Applause.] In the religious as well as in the social zone of our faculties, only love can smite all the chords with might, or smite the chord of self into invisibility and music. *But the love which can do this is not admiration only; it is adoration.*

Theodore Parker's absolute religion fails to distinguish properly between the admiration and the adoration of the Ineffable Holy Person which Parker admits that the moral law reveals.

1. Admiration does not always imply a full and vivid view of the Infinite Holiness of the Infinite Oughtness revealed by the moral law. Adoration always does imply this.

2. Admiration does not always imply a glad self-commitment of the soul to the Infinite Holiness. Adoration always does.

3. Admiration usually has but a fragmentary view of the Divine attributes as revealed in the nature of things. Adoration has, or is willing to have, a full view.

4. Admiration may give pleasure for a time. Adoration gives bliss.

5. Admiration may have delight in only a few of

God's attributes. Adoration is supreme delight in all God's attributes.

6. Admiration of God is often all that is found, or all that it is thought necessary to require, in the distinctively literary or poetic schemes of sceptical religious thought. Adoration, however, and not merely admiration, of an Infinitely Holy Person revealed by the moral law, is scientifically known to be necessary to the peace of the soul with the nature of things.

What are the signs of this error in Parker's writings?

1. Theodore Parker made only a fragmentary use of the intuitions or self-evident truths of the soul.

2. Hence his view of that portion of the divine nature which may be known to man was fragmentary.

3. The inadequate emphasis he laid on the fact of sin shows how fragmentary this view was.

4. Parker's fragmentary view of the Divine nature is shown in his constant undervaluing of the nature of things as it is faithfully represented in the Old Testament.

Goethe's literary insight, you will probably think, was quite as keen as Matthew Arnold's is; and he, long before Arnold, applied purely literary tests to the Hebrew Scriptures, as religious science herself has been doing for a hundred years. The Old Testament is not sterner than the nature of things. It is amazing that Matthew Arnold believes his famous literary test to be a new one. Goethe said, and Parker used in his earlier career to quote the words admiringly, " The Hebrew Scriptures stand so happily combined together, that, even out of the most diverse elements, the feeling of a whole still rises before us. They are complete enough to satisfy, fragmentary enough to excite, barbarous enough to arouse, tender enough to appease." (See FROTHINGHAM'S *Parker*, p. 56.)

The Old Testament Scriptures out of date? Not till the nature of things is! [Applause.] I rode once from a noon on the Dead Sea, through moonlight on the Mar Saba gorges, to Bethlehem in the morning light. I passed through the scenes in which many of David's psalms had their origin, so far as human causes brought them into existence. On horseback I climbed slowly and painfully out of that scorched, ghastly hollow in which the Salt Lake lies. I found myself, as I ascended, passing through a gnarled, smitten, volcanic region, and often at the edge or in the depth of ravines deeper than that eloquent shaft yonder on Bunker Hill is high. At a place where, no doubt, David had often searched for his flocks, I found the famous convent of Mar Saba clinging to the side of its stupendous ravine, and I lay down there and slept until the same sun rose which David saw. I looked northward from above Mar Saba, and saw Jerusalem above me yet to the north; for I had been ascending from a spot greatly below the level of the Mediterranean. As I drew near Bethlehem, through brown wheat-fields in which a woman called Ruth once gleaned, I opened and read the book which will bear her name yet to thousands of years to come.

Johnson, you remember, once read that book in London, and moved a parlor full of people to tears by it, and to curiosity enough to ask who was the author of that beautiful pastoral. In my saddle there in Syria I was moved as Johnson's hearers were in London; but when I opened the Psalms, one by one, and looked back over the ravines toward the Dead Sea, and northward toward Jerusalem, and upon the hill of Bethlehem, to which all nations after a gaze of nineteen hundred years in duration, were looking yet, and at that season sending pilgrims; when I remembered how that terraced hill of olive-gardens had influenced human history as no other spot on the globe has done, and that in God's government of this planet there are no accidents; when I took up the astounding harp of Isaiah, and turned through the list of the prophets to find mysterious passage after passage predicting what would come and what has come; and when I thought of those critics under the western sky who would saw asunder the Old Testament and the New, and put into the shade those Scriptures which Goethe calls a unit in themselves, and which are doubly a unit when united with the New Testament, I remembered Him who, on the way to Emmaus, opened the Old Testament Scriptures, and with them made men's hearts burn. [Applause.]

God and the nature of things have no cross-purposes. Truth works well, and what works well is truth.

If we are out of harmony with the nature of things, we may be scientifically certain that we are out of harmony with God.

Only a religion consisting of delight in all God's attributes, or adoration of the whole nature of things as representative of the Divine Nature, can satisfy the demands of self-evident truth.

With multitudes of other careless students of the nature of things, Theodore Parker taught the admiration rather than the adoration of God.

I do not forget those prayers of this man, which seem to ascend always as into a dateless noon of mercy, and I do not deny the existence of that dateless noon; but, even if I were to forget, uncounted ages would yet remember that the prayers which caused great drops of blood to fall down to the ground were not quite in that mood, and that no doubt He who offered them knew the full reach of the Divine Mercy, and that it would go as far as the Divine Justice can, but that there are moral impossibilities to a Holy Being.

My friends, you may do as you please; but I, for one, will not take my leap into the Unseen Holy without looking for the truth around the whole horizon of inquiry; and I find that the most sceptical of you are agreed that there is a stern and an infinitely tender nature of things; and that, even if God exists not, you must be reconciled with the nature of things; and that, if God exists, you must yet be reconciled with it, for God himself has no cross-purposes with it.

If a vivid view of the nature of things produced this bloody sweat, perhaps you and I ought not to dream through life, thinking that every fall is a fall upward, and that it can never be too late to mend. *All history proves that such a faith does not work well.* A faith that does not work well is scientifically known to be out of harmony with natural law.

What effect arises by natural law in the soul when a man is brought to a vivid sense of the nearness of the Holy Person the moral law reveals? This question I, for one, am anxious should be investigated in the light of exact research; for the use of the scientific method in answering this inquiry opens the door to the proof that Christianity is the religion of science.

1. The more a man has of the religion demanded by the nature of things, that is, the more adoration he has of the Infinite Holiness of the Infinite Oughtness revealed by the moral law, the more he is thrown into silence as to his own righteousness, into self-condemnation, and into unrest and fear as to the future effect of his past sins.

Gentlemen, I affirm that this is a fair rendering of the history of the human heart age after age. When a man comes near to God, his mood is not that of self-justification. Wait until eternity breathes on your cheek, wait until you come face to face with Somewhat in conscience' that Shakspeare says makes cowards of us all, and then ask whether the Infinite Holiness of the moral law will be altogether satisfactory to you. Put the question here and now, whether we, in our characters as they stand at this moment, should be happy if we were in heaven with our characters unchanged. Whitefield asked that question on Boston Common yonder in 1740. . It has been asked in every century for eighteen hundred years, and now is asked by science; and every one in his senses, when listening to the still small voice, has said, "As for me, I am the son of a man of unclean lips, and I am a man of unclean lips, and in my own righteousness I cannot stand alone before God." What are we to make of this action of human nature? It is a fact, and it is an immeasurably significant fact. That is the way of history; and I defy any man to show that I am not true to the unforced outcome of human nature outside of all the creeds, when I say that a view of all God's attributes humiliates man, puts him out of conceit with his own righteousness, and brings him more and more, even after he has reformed, into fear lest it may not be well with him, because there is a past behind him which ought to be covered. We are made so; and, when a religion will not work well in those deep hours in which we see the structure of our own souls, I am afraid to take it in my lighter hours. Addison said that a religion should work well in three places, if it is good for any thing, on death-beds, in our highest moments of emotional illumination, and when we are keenest rationally. A religion does not work well anywhere unless in all these three places. Take your scheme of thought that assumes that it is never too late to mend, or that every fall is a fall upward, and bring it face to face with these deepest expressions of human nature, age after age. Does it work well there in these deepest moments? If I find, that, age after age, a scheme of thought is not likely to make men better, is not improving society, is not taking hold of bad lives and making them good, that is for me a sufficient proof that it is out of harmony with natural law. If, in the long course of experience, a scheme of thought does not make me better, does not put a bridle upon passion, does not lift me into harmony with all the divine attributes, I know from that fact scientifically that it is out of harmony with the Infinite Oughtness which stands behind the moral law. [Applause.]

2. The only conception of God's character given under heaven or among men, by which a man who worships all God's attributes can be at peace, is Christ's conception.

3. The superiority of Christianity to all schemes of natural religion is, that it presents the idea of God as an Incarnate God and as an Atoning God, and of personal love to that Person as the means of the purification of the world.

Christianity does not teach that personal demerit is taken off from us, and put upon our Lord. Such transference is an impossibility in the nature of things. But I hold that Christianity, with the Atonement as its central truth, matches the nature of things, and turns exactly in the wards of the human soul. It has, as a theory of religious truth, a scientific beauty absolutely beyond all comment. The returned deserter, knowing his own permanent and unremovable personal demerit, may yet be allowed to escape the penalty of the law by the substitution of the king's chastisement for the deserter's punishment; and then that deserter, looking on his king as both his Saviour and Lord, needs no other motive to loyalty than the memory of his unspeakable condescension, justice, and love. That memory gives rise to adoration. Whether or not this scheme of thought be the correct one, I am not asking you now to determine; but certainly it is the most moving, the most natural, and the most qualified to regenerate human nature, of all the schemes the world has seen. I speak of it here and now only as an intellectual system, and affirm, in the name of the cool precision of the scientific method, that *Christianity, and it only, as a scheme of thought, shows how man may look on all God's attributes, and be at peace. It and it only provides for our deliverance from both the love of sin and the guilt of sin.* Merely as a school of ideas adapted to the soul's inmost wants, Christianity is as much above all other philosophy in merit as the noon is more radiant than a rushlight. "The cross," said a successor of Theodore Parker to me the other day, "is full of the nature of things." God be praised that this incisively scientific sentence has come from the lips of a successor of Theodore Parker! "The cross is not an after-thought." We are to love a God who from eternity to eternity is our Redeemer; and, looking on him as such, we are to take him affectionately as both Saviour and Lord. Christianity includes all ethics; it teaches adoration before all the divine attributes; it is a philosophy; it is an art; it is a growth; and it is also a revelation of the nature of things which has no variableness nor shadow of turning. But its central thought is that of a Holy Person revealed by the moral law, and at once Redeemer and Lord, and of love for that Person as the means, and the only possible effective means, for the purification of the world. God as an atoning God, God as revealed in history, the Cross full of the nature of things, the personal love of Infinite Perfection as a regenerating bath, this is the beautiful and awful which has triumphed, and will continue to triumph. [Applause.]

X.
THE TRINITY AND TRITHEISM.

THE SIXTY-EIGHTH LECTURE IN THE BOSTON MONDAY LECTURESHIP, IN TREMONT TEMPLE MARCH 6.

"οὐκ ἔχω προσεικάσαι,
πάντ' ἐπισταθμώμενος,
πλὴν Διός, εἰ τὸ μάταν ἀπὸ φροντίδος ἄχθος
χρὴ βαλεῖν ἐτητύμως.
οὐδ' ὅστις πάροιθεν ἦν μέγας,
παμμάχῳ θράσει βρύων,
οὐδὲν ἂν λέξαι πρὶν ὤν,
ὃς δ' ἔπειτ' ἔφυ, τρια-
κτῆρος οἴχεται τυχών."

ÆSCHYLUS: *Agamemnon*, 163-171.

" Simul quoque cum beatis videamus
 Glorianter vultum Tuum, Christe Deus,
 Gaudium quod est immensum atque probum,
 Sæcula per infinita sæculorum."

Rhythm. Eccl.

X.

THE TRINITY AND TRITHEISM.

PRELUDE ON CURRENT EVENTS.

CIVIL-SERVICE reform is to-day to be nominally, and perhaps really, crowned in Washington. Both political parties have demanded on paper the reformation of our system of giving all political spoils to political victors; and that reformation we can now have, if Congress and the people are agreed. The executive and legislative powers and popular sentiment once united, any reform can be carried in the United States. If signs commonly thought sure do not mislead, it may be asserted that popular sentiment and the Executive are now united in favor of what is known as civil-service reform. This is the best news since Gettysburg. The question now is, whether the upper and nether mill-stones of executive and popular power can grind to pieces any selfish or obtuse opposition in Congress, or among the placemen of party to this righteous and momentous cause. In expressing a hope that we may return from the Jacksonian to the Jeffersonian and Washingtonian policy in regard to our civil service, I shall offend no man's prejudices. I assume that every one who is disappointed in the result of the presidential contest would be sincerely glad to have all that was promised in the Democratic platform carried out in our politics. I shall also assume, with equal audacity, that every member of the political party now in power holds sincerely the propositions announced in the letter of acceptance of him who is to-day inaugurated as the President of a people who will number fifty millions before his term of office expires.

Scholars in politics assuredly are agreed that resistance to the crescent and now haughty evils which have arisen from the application of Jacksonian principles to our national politics cannot be made too swift and decisive. I do not couple Jefferson's name with Jackson's; for the truth is, that we are now beginning to go back from the democracy of Jackson to that of Jefferson. The action of the latter, so far as the civil service is concerned, was one with the practice of Washington and Adams, Madison and Monroe. Never forget, what cannot be too often repeated, that Washington, in all the eight years of his administration, removed only nine men from office; Adams, only nine; Jefferson, thirty-nine, but none for political reasons; Madison, nine; Monroe, five; John Quincy Adams, two; Jackson, according to his opponents, two thousand, and, according to his own admission, six hundred and ninety. (See GREG, *Rocks Ahead, Appendix on American Politics.*)

Some of us younger men, who never saw in use in the civil service any other than our present spoils system, think that the arrangement by which all political spoils are to be given to political victors is a natural law, and originated in that time when the morning stars sang together — not for joy. My State of New York, empire in both commerce and iniquity, — God save her! — saw the origination of the spoils system in the factious quarrels between the ins and outs among the Clintons and Livingstons, from 1800 to 1830. Sitting over the mahogany of their dinner-tables, these great aristocratic families of the Hudson distributed offices among their adherents according to the principle that to party victors belong party spoils. Rotation in office began to be practised in New York and Pennsylvania near the beginning of the century. It was Jan. 24, 1832, when Marcy, making a speech in the Senate in favor of sending Van Buren to England as an ambassador, first defended in Congress the principle that to political victors belong political spoils. It was Aaron Burr himself, who, in 1815, writing a letter to his son-in-law, Allston of South Carolina, first suggested for President Andrew Jackson, — one of the bravest, but not one of the broadest, men the world ever saw. No doubt, if Jackson were alive to-day, he would be among the first to seize by the throat the serpent which came out of the egg which was hatched in our national politics in his administration, although laid first in New-York State. Civil-service reform takes patronage from party, and gives it to the people. It was between 1830 and 1840 that the initiative of the people died out in our national politics. While we were busy with an opening West and with anthracite coal and railways, and modern political newspapers, and the electric telegraph, and California, the spoils system grew up. An astounding civil war drew on apace. We had no time to study minor dangers; it was necessary to make Congress strong.

In our first centennial year we had eighty thousand, and, before a second or third centennial, we shall probably have two hundred thousand or three hundred thousand civil-service offices. Are we to follow the spoils system, and turn out or put in that number of partisan placemen with every change of administration? If so, we shall do well to remember Macaulay's predictions, that, when the United States have a population of two hundred to the square mile, the Jeffersonian parts of our polity will produce fatal effects. If you think the Jeffersonian will not, ask yourself, face to face with recent events, whether the Jacksonian will. Massachusetts has not yet a population of two hundred to the square mile. But what if the whole land were as thickly settled as Massachusetts, and we were to manage every thing as now, by the Jacksonian rule, that to political victors belong all political spoils?

Twice our land has been washed in blood in the first hundred years of its history; and yet, after that washing, Lowell calls America the land of broken promise. There is not on the globe a more patriotic poet than he; and you may count the graves of his relatives who fell in the civil war, if you will go yonder to the eloquent sods the spring is kissing in Mount Auburn. Your Lowell says, and the poem is fit to be read in Boston on this inauguration noon:

> " The world turns mild. Democracy, they say,
> Rounds the sharp knobs of character away.
> The Ten Commandments had a meaning once,
> Felt in their bones by least considerate men,
> Because behind them public conscience stood,
> And without wincing made their mandates good.
> But now that statesmanship is just a way
> To dodge the primal curse, and make it pay,
> Since office means a kind of patent drill
> To force an entrance to the nation's till;
> And peculation something rather less
> Risky than if you spelt it with an S,
> Now that to steal by law is grown an art,
> Whom rogues the sires, their milder sons call smart."
> *Tempora Mutantur.*

[Applause.]

Remembering that this President who is inaugurated to-day went into the civil war, and brought back alive only a third of the officers who enlisted under him; remembering that he, at least, has not corruptly or even anxiously sought his present high position, however much there may have been of greed and fraud behind him in the organization that has elected him; remembering that he has a character, a new thing, rather, in high places; remembering that he left Ohio as Lincoln did Illinois, asking the prayers of all men that the Eternal Providence might watch over his course; remembering that there are things in our land which war could not settle, and which only wise, victorious, patient politics can arrange in a manner to satisfy North and South, East and West alike; remembering especially that this party which the present Chief Magistrate represents has been sixteen years in power, and therefore has presumably had a great deal of temptation [applause], shall we not unite, not only our prayer, but our watching, and send a keen atmosphere of both from the four winds, to breathe on our legislative power, till the civil-service practice of Washington and Jefferson shall start up as a flame from its dying embers, and, fed by the colossal fuel of our new political conditions, become once more the light and the glad fireside of the land; and Macaulay and observant Europe, as they gaze into our future, can have on this point no more ground for fear? [Applause.]

THE LECTURE.

There is a dim twilight of religious experience in which the soul easily mistakes Ossa and Parnassus for Sinai and Calvary. My feeling is, that orthodoxy itself lives much of the time in this undispersed twilight; and that the unscientific and lawless liberalism of many half-educated people who have lost the Master's whip of small cords, believe in æsthetic, but not in moral law, and proclaim, that, in the last analysis, there is in this universe nothing to be feared (Dr.

Bartol says so), and therefore, we must add, nothing to be loved! — is always in an earlier and deeper shadow of that misleading haze. The gray, brindled dawn is better than night; but the risen sun is better than the gray, brindled dawn. We must startle mere æsthetics and literary religiosity out of its dream that it is religion, by exhibiting before it the difference between the admiration and the adoration of the attributes of the Holy Person the moral law reveals. If any who are orthodox in their thoughts worship in their imagination three different beings, they, too, must be startled from this remnant of Paganism by a stern use of the scientific method.

As Carlyle says of America, so I of this hushed, reverent discussion, — do not judge of the structure while the scaffolding is up. A glimpse only of the opening of the unfathomable theme which the distinction between the Tri-unity of the Divine Nature and Tritheism suggests can be given here and now; and more than this will be expected by no scholar. Reserving qualifications for later occasions, I purposely present to-day only an outline unobscured by detail. I know what I venture in definition and illustration; but I am asking no one to take my opinions. Nevertheless, in order yet further to save time, I am to cast myself abruptly into the heart of this topic, and to give you personal conviction. After all, that is what serious men want from each other; and the utterance of it is not egotism in you or in me. It is the shortest way of coming at men's hearts, and it is sometimes the shortest way in which to come at men's heads, to tell what you personally are willing to take the leap into the Unseen, depending upon.

What is the definition of the Trinity?

1. The Father, the Son, and the Holy Ghost are one and only one God.
2. Each has a peculiarity incommunicable to the others.
3. Neither is God without the others.
4. Each, with the others, is God.

That I suppose to be the standard definition; and, if you will examine it, you will find it describing neither three separate individualities, nor yet three mere modes of manifestation; that is, neither tritheism nor modalism. In God are *not* three wills, three consciences, three intellects, three sets of affections. The first of all the religious truths of exact research is that the Lord our God is one God. It is the immemorial doctrine of the Christian ages, that there are not three Gods, but only one God (Athanasian Creed). He is one substance, and in that one substance are three subsistences; but the subsistences are not individualities. All the great symbols teach decisively that we must not unify the subsistences; but with equal decisiveness they affirm that we must not divide the substance. In our present low estate as human, we find by the experience of centuries that we do well to heed both these injunctions, and to look on the Divine Nature on all the sides on which it has revealed itself, if we would not fall into the narrowness of materialism on the one hand, or into the vague ways of tritheism or pantheism on the other.

How shall we make clear in our intellectual and emotional experiences the truth of the Trinity, and at the same time keep ourselves in the attitude of those who worship one God, and who therefore do not break, or wish to break, with science, and yet in the position of those who, in the one substance, worship three subsistencies, and therefore do not break, or wish to break, with the very significant record of the most fruitful portion of the church through eighteen hundred years? For one, accepting the definition of the Trinity which I have now given as neither tritheistic nor modalistic,—if the learned men here will allow me for once to use technical language,— I personally find no difficulty in this doctrine in the shape of self-contradiction in either thought or terms; and I find infinite advantages in it when I wish to conjoin biblical and scientific truth as a transfiguration for life.

It is sometimes despairingly said, that the doctrine of the Trinity cannot be illustrated; and this is true. It is the proverb of philosophy, that no comparison walks on four feet; and what I am about to say you will take as intended by me to exhibit only the parallelisms which I point out. I am responsible for no unmentioned point in a comparison. No doubt you can find as many places where the illustration I am to use will not agree with the definition as I can places where it does agree. Nevertheless, after dwelling on perhaps a hundred other illustrations, my own thoughts oftenest, and with most of reverence, come back to this.

Take the mysterious, palpitating radiance which at this instant streams through the solar windows of this Temple, and may we not say, for the sake of illustration, that it is one substance? Can you not affirm, however, that there are in it three subsistencies? It would be possible for me, by a prism here, to produce the seven colors on a screen yonder. I should have color there, and heat here, and there would be luminousness everywhere. But in color is a property incommunicable to mere luminousness or to heat. In luminousness is a property incommunicable to mere heat or to color. In heat is a property incommunicable to mere color or to luminousness. These three — luminousness, color, heat — are, however, one solar radiance. Heat subsists in the solar radiance, and color subsists in the solar radiance, and light subsists in the solar radiance. The three are one; but they are not one in the same sense in which they are three.

It is one of the inexcusable mistakes of a silly kind of scepticism, which no one here holds, that there are in the Trinity three persons in the literal or colloquial sense of that word. Sometimes with tears, and sometimes with laughter, one pauses over this astounding passage, printed in his manhood by Thomas Paine, in his Age of Reason; and yet what he heard read was, I presume, an atrociously careless orthodox discussion.

"I well remember, when about seven or eight years of age, hearing a sermon read by a relation of mine, who was a great devotee of the church, upon the subject of what is called *redemption by the death of the Son of God.* After the sermon was ended, I went into the garden; and, as I was going down the garden-steps (for I perfectly recollect the spot), I revolted at the recollection of what I had heard, and thought to myself that it was making God Almighty act like a passionate man that killed his son when he could not revenge himself any other way; and, as I was sure a man would be hanged that did such a thing, I could not see for what purpose they preached such sermons. This was not one of those kind of thoughts that had any thing in it of childish levity: it was to me a serious reflection, arising from the idea I had, that God was too good to do such an action, and also too almighty to be under any necessity of doing it. I believe in the same manner at this moment. . . . The Christian mythology has five deities; there is God the Father, God the Son, God the Holy Ghost, the God Providence, and the Goddess Nature. But the Christian story of God the Father putting his Son to death, or employing people to do it (for that is the plain language of the story), cannot be told by a parent to a child; and to tell him that it was done to make mankind happier and better is making the story still worse, as if mankind could be improved by the example of murder " (*Age of Reason,* part i.).

There is nothing in Paine's Age of Reason worth glancing at now, except this curious paragraph, in which he details the circumstances of the life-long unconscious obtuseness and ignorance out of which arose his opposition to Christianity. Possibly, if he had understood the distinction between the Trinity in God's nature and tritheism, this sharp and crackling pamphleteer for freedom, in spite of his narrow brow and coarse fibre, would not have fallen into this amazing error, which, according to his own account, underlay all his subsequent career as an infidel. Three separate beings, he thought, Christianity teaches us to believe exist in one God, and one enraged person of these three had murdered another person.

But scholars as a mass, following St. Augustine, centuries before poor Paine's day, copiously affirmed that the word *person* in the discussion of the Trinity does not mean what it does in colloquial speech. The word in its technical use is fifteen hundred years old; and it means in that use now what it meant at first.

How commonplace is St. Augustine's remark, repeated by Calvin, that this term was adopted because of the poverty of the Latin tongue! Everybody of authority tells us, if you care for scholarly statement, that three *persons* never meant, in the standard discussions of this truth, three *personalities;* for these would be three Gods. This Latin word *persons* is incalculably misleading in popular use on this theme. For one, I never employ it, although willing to use it if it is understood as it was by those who invented the term. Let us use Archbishop Whateley's word "subsistence;" for that is the equivalent of the carefully-chosen, sharply-cut, Greek term "hypostasis" (*Note to* WHATELEY'S *Treatise on Logic*). We had better say there are in one substance three subsistences, and not mislead our generation, with its heads in newspapers and ledgers, by using a phrase that was meant to be current only among scholars. All these scholars will tell you that it is no evasion of the difficulties of this theme for me to throw out of this discussion at once the word *persons* as misleading; for that word had originally no such meaning in the Latin tongue as the word *person* has in our own. Cicero says, *Ego unus, sustineo tres personas:* I, being one, sustain three characters, — my own, that of my client, and that of the judge. Our English language at this point is, as the Latin was not, rich enough to match the old Greek. With Liddon's Bampton Lectures on " The Divinity of our Lord," the best English book on this theme, though not exhaustive of it, let us say, " One substance and three subsistences," and thus go back to the Greek phrase, and be clear.

Can the four propositions of the definition I have given be paralleled by an illustration?

1. Sunlight, the rainbow, and the heat of sunlight, are one solar radiance.

2. Each has a peculiarity incommunicable to the others.

3. Neither is full solar radiance without the others.

4. Each with the others is such solar radiance.

Sunlight, rainbow, heat, one solar radiance; Father, Son, Holy Ghost, one God!

1. As the rainbow shows what light is when unfolded, so Christ reveals the nature of God.

2. As all of the rainbow is sunlight, so all of Christ's divine soul is God!

3. As the rainbow was when the light was, or from eternity, so Christ was when the Father was, or from eternity.

4. As the bow may be on the earth and the sun in the sky, and yet the solar radiance remain undivided, so God may remain in heaven, and appear on earth as Christ, and his oneness not be divided.

5. As the perishable raindrop is used in the revelation of the rainbow, so was Christ's body in the revelation to men of God in Christ.

6. As at the same instant the sunlight is itself, and also the rainbow and heat, so at the same moment Christ is both himself and the Father, and both the Father and the Holy Ghost.

7. As solar heat has a peculiarity incommunicable to solar color, and solar color a peculiarity incommunicable to solar light, and solar light a peculiarity incommunicable to either solar color or solar heat, so each of the three — the Father, Son, and Holy Ghost — has a peculiarity incommunicable to either of the others.

8. But as solar light, heat, and color are one solar radiance, so the Father, Son, and Holy Ghost are one God.

9. As neither solar heat, light, nor color is itself without the aid of the others, so neither Father, Son, nor Holy Ghost is God without the others.

10. As solar heat, light, and color are each solar radiance, so Father, Son, and Holy Ghost are each God.

11. As the solar rainbow fades from sight, and its light continues to exist, so Christ ceases to be manifest, and yet is present.

12. As the rainbow issues from sunlight, and re-

turns to the general bosom of the radiance of the sky, so Christ comes from the Father, appears for a while, and returns, and yet is not absent from the earth.

13. As the influence of the heat is that of the light of the sun, so are the operations of the Holy Spirit Christ's continued life.

14. As is the relation of all vegetable growths to solar light and heat, so is the relation of all religious growths in general history, in the church, and in the individual, to the Holy Spirit, a present Christ.

It was my fortune once, on an October Sabbath evening, to stand alone at the grave of Wordsworth, in green Grasmere, in the English lake district, and to read there the Ode on Immortality, which your Emerson calls the highest-water mark of modern poetry and philosophy. While my eyes were fastened on the page, the sun was setting behind the gnarled, inaccessible English cliffs, not far away to the west, and a colossal rainbow was spread over the azure of the sky, and the glowing purple and brown of the heathered hills in the east. A light rain fell on me, and with my own tears wet the pages of the poet. What, now, if some one, as I worshipped there, had come to me, in a holy of holies in my life, and had said roughly, in Thomas Paine's way, "You believe in five Gods; you are not scientific"? Or what if some one had said, in Parker's way, "The perfection of God has never been accepted by any sect in the Christian world. In the Ecclesiastic conception of Deity there is a fourth person, the

Devil, as much a part of Deity as either Son or Holy Ghost" (WEISS's *Life of Parker*, vol. ii. p. 470). "Vicarious atonement teaches salvation without morality, only by belief in absurd teaching" (Ibid., p. 497).

"According to the popular theology there are three acknowledged persons in the Godhead. God the Father is made to appear remarkable for three things, — great power, great selfishness, and great destructiveness. The Father is the grimmest object in the universe" (*Sermons on Theism*, p. 101). "He is the Draco of the universe, — more cruel than Odin or Baal, — the author of sin, but its unforgiving avenger. Men rush from the Father; they flee to the Son." "The popular theology makes Jesus a God, and does not tell us of God now near at hand. Science must lay his kingly head in the dust, Reason veil her majestic countenance, Conscience bow him to the earth, Affection keep silence, when the priest uplifts the Bible" (*Discourses on Religion*, pp. 425–427).

How would all that speech of the Parkers and the Paines have jarred upon my soul, if standing there alone in a strange land, and at the grave of Wordsworth, I had heard the profane collision of their accusations with the holy sentences of this seer, fed from the cradle to the tomb upon Christian truth! If, at Wordsworth's grave, disturbed by such ghoulish attack, I had needed a spell to disperse the accusations, what better *Procul, procul, este profani* could I have chosen than these words, once uttered in this city by a renowned teacher of this accused theology, a man of whom it might be said, as he once said of Jonathan Edwards, that he might have been the first poet of his nation, if he had not chosen to be its first theologian! [Applause.]

A majestic discourse delivered at the installation of the revered pastor of the Old South Church yonder says, " Other men may be alone; but the Christian, wherever he moves, is near to his Master. Every effect is the result of some free will; but many effects within and without us are not produced by a created will: therefore they are produced by an uncreated. On the deep sea, under the venerable oak, in the pure air of the mountain-top, the Christian communes with the Father of spirits, who is the Saviour of men. All ethical axioms are his revelation of himself to his children. Their innocent joys are his words of good cheer. Their deserved sorrows are his loud rebukes."

In these words of Professor Park, a benighted believer in three Gods, as you say [applause], is God afar off? Are there three Gods here? Does Science bow her head, Affection grow dumb, Reason muffle her face, as this priest lifts up the Bible?

As the rainbow shows the inner structure of the light, so the character of our Lord shows the inner moral nature of God, so far as that can be known to man. A rainbow is unravelled light, is it not? It was assuredly better for me at Wordsworth's grave to look on the bow I saw in the East than to gaze on the white radiance that fell on the poet's page, when I wished to behold the fullest glory of the light. So assuredly it is better for us to gaze on God's character as revealed in Christ than on God's character as revealed in his works merely, if we would understand God's nature. As the rainbow is unravelled light, so Christ is unravelled God. At Wordsworth's grave I might have heard these hoarse voices from the Paines and the Parkers, and these softer, and I think more penetratingly human ones from the Wordsworths and the Parks; but, in the name of the scientific method, it would have been impossible not to have asserted in my soul that the God who was revealed in Christ was, and is, and is to come; for there is but one God, and he was, and is, and is to come; and, therefore, when the bow faded from the East, I did not think that it had ceased to be. It had not been annihilated; it had been revealed for a while, and, disappearing, it was received back into the bosom of the general radiance, and yet continued to fall upon the earth. In every beam of white light there is potentially all the color which we find unravelled in the rainbow; and so in all the pulsations in the will of God the Father in his works, exist the pulsations of the heart of Him who wept over Jerusalem, and on whose bosom once the beloved disciple leaned; for there is but one God, who was, and is, and is to come; and on the same bosom we bow our heads whenever we bow our foreheads upon that Sinai within us which we call the moral law. [Applause.] The Holy Spirit to me is Christ's continued life.

But you say, my friends, that this may be philosophical, but that it is not biblical truth. You affirm that I teach myself this by science rather than by Scripture. Gentlemen, under the noon of New-England philosophical and biblical culture, and in presence of I know not how many who dissent, I ask you to decide for yourselves what the Scriptures really teach as to the unity of the three subsistences in that Divine Nature which was, and is, and is to come. Assuredly you will be ready, in the name of literary science, to cast at least one searching glance upon this whole theme from the point of view of exclusively biblical statement.

" It is expedient for you that I go away. I have yet many things to say unto you. I will not leave you orphans. I am coming to you. A little while and ye shall not see me, and again a little while and ye shall see me, because I go to the Father." They who heard these sentences said, " A little while and ye shall not see me, and again a little while and ye shall see me, and because I go to the Father? What is this he saith? We cannot tell what he saith." But there came a later day, when He who had made that promise breathed upon them, and said, "Receive ye the gift of the Holy Ghost." We shall not be here, all of us will be mute, and most of us forgotten, when, in a better age, the meaning of that symbolic act of the Author of Christianity is fathomed.

Next there came a day when there was a sound as of a rushing, mighty wind; and this filled all the house where they who had witnessed that act were sitting. This is but the experience of many nations since then, — the rushing sound of a new influence in human history, quickening human consciences, transforming bad lives into good, but, until that time, never felt in the world in deluges, although it had appeared in streams. When that influence came, what was the interpretation put upon it by the scriptural writers? Peter, standing up, said, "We heard, from him whom we know that God has raised from the dead, the promise of the Holy Ghost. He hath shed forth this; therefore, let Jerusalem know assuredly that God hath made him Lord." I call that Peter's colossal *therefore*. It is the strongest word in the first oration delivered in the defence of Christianity. The Holy Spirit was promised; it has been poured out: therefore, let those who receive it know that the power behind natural law — our Lord who was, and is, and is to come — is now breathing upon the centuries as he breathed upon us symbolically. He has shed forth this: therefore, let all men know assuredly that God hath made him Lord. When they who were assembled in Jerusalem at that time heard this *therefore*, they were pricked in the heart.

I affirm that it is incontrovertible, that the New-Testament writers, everywhere with Stephen, gaze steadfastly into heaven, and behold our Lord, not in Galilee, not on the Mount of Olives, but at the right hand of the Father. Our imagination always looks eastward through England, as through the East window of a cathedral; and so we look out through vapor sometimes, through literalness, or through materialistic haze, thicker than vapor occasionally; and we have not strength of imagination or fervor of spirit enough to understand this literature of the East, on the face of which the world has gazed eighteen hundred years, and seen its face to be like that of Stephen, as the face of an angel, and from the same cause. The whole New Testament, being full of the Holy Ghost, gazes, not as England and America do, into Gethsemane, or upon any sacred mount, but into heaven, and beholds our Lord at the right hand of the Father. I have bowed down upon the Mount of Olives, I have had unreportable experiences in the Garden of Gethsemane, and on the banks of Jordan, and on the white, sounding shore of Galilee, and on Lebanon, and on Carmel, and on Tabor; and God forbid that I should underrate at all a religion that reverences sacred places; but, of these sacred places the New Testament proclaims, "He is not here: he has arisen and is ascended." It nowhere exhibits our narrowness of outlook.

What if, under the dome of St. Peter's, there were but four windows? What if children were brought up to look out yonder upon the Apennines, and here upon the Mediterranean, and there upon the Coliseum, and here upon St. Onofrio's oak, under which Tasso sung? If children were brought up before these windows, and did not pass from one to the other, they might possibly think the outlook from each one was Italy; and so it is; but it is only a part of Italy. We are poor children, brought up, some of us, before the window of science, some of us before the window of art, some of us before the window of politics, some of us before the window of biblical inculcation; and we say in petulant tones to each other, each at his accustomed outlook, " This is Italy." What is Italy? Sweep off the dome, and answer, " There is but one sky." [Applause.] And that and all beneath it is Italy.

As a fact in literature, it must be affirmed that this is the central thought of the New-Testament Scriptures.

We find, that, when one called Saul of Tarsus journeyed to Damascus, — this is trite, because eighteen hundred years have heard it, and the trite is the important thing in history, — he heard, from a light above the brightness of this noon, the words, " I am Jesus;" and so, later on, Paul wrote, that " we, beholding, as in a glass, the glory of the Lord, are changed with the same image from glory to glory as by the Lord the Spirit." "The Spirit is the Lord," was St. Augustine's reading of Paul's words.

So, in the last pages of Revelation, I find that he who was the beloved disciple was in the Spirit on the Lord's Day, and that he beheld " one whose voice was like unto the sound of many waters, and whose countenance was as the sun shineth in his strength." " When I saw him," says this great poet and prophet and apostle, " I, who have been called a son of thunder; I who, when Cerinthus was in the same bath with me, cried out, Away, thou heretic! I who have been ready at any time to suffer martyrdom, — I fell at his feet as dead. He laid his right hand on me, saying unto me, fear not; I am the first and the last; I am he that liveth, and was dead; behold I am alive forevermore, and have the keys of life and of death."

It is significant beyond comment, that our Lord was often called "The Spirit," and "The Spirit of God," by the earlier Christian writers. "The Son is the Holy Spirit" is a common expression. Ignatius said, "Christ is the Immaculate Spirit" (*Ad Smym. init.*). Tertullian wrote, "The Spirit of God and the Reason of God — Word of Reason, and Reason and Spirit of Word — Jesus Christ our Lord, who is both the one and the other" (*De Orat. init.*) Cyprian and Irenæus said, "He is the Holy Spirit." (See DELITZSCH'S *System of Biblical Psychology.*)

Neander, in paraphrase of Peter's oration, says, in summarizing the New-Testament literature, "From the extraordinary appearances which have filled you with astonishment, you perceive, that, in his glorified state, he is now operating with divine energy among those who believe in him. The heavenly Father has promised that the Messiah shall fill all who believe on him with the power of the Divine Spirit, and this promise is now being fulfilled. Learn, then, from these events, in which you behold the prophecies of the Old Testament fulfilled, the nothingness of all that you have attempted against him, and know that God has exalted Him whom you crucified to be Messiah, the ruler of God's kingdom; and that, through Divine Power, he will overawe all his enemies." (NEANDER, *Planting of Christianity*, Bohn's edition, i. 19. Summary of Peter's speech in Acts ii.)

So Alford writes, " Christ is the Spirit; is identical with the Holy Spirit, not personally nor essentially, but (as is shown by the spirit of the Lord following) in this department of his divine working : Christ here is the Spirit of Christ" (*Remarks on* 2 Cor. iii. 17).

Lange, writing on the same passage of this literature, adds, " We find here such an identification of Christ and the Holy Spirit, that the Lord to whom the heart turns is in no practical respect different from the Holy Spirit received in conversion. Christ is virtually the Spirit. The Holy Spirit is his spirit " (LANGE, 2 Cor. iii. 17, 18).

What if Peter at Antioch had beheld the earliest triumphs of Christianity under persecution, and had heard the story of the martyrdoms which became the seed of the church, and caused Christians to be called by that name, and that shot through with hope the unspeakable despair of Roman Paganism as by the first rays of the dawn, could he not, looking on Lebanon and Tabor, on Jerusalem and Galilee, have said, " He hath shed forth this advance of Christianity in human affairs? God has a plan, and he thus reveals it. God is giving triumph to Christianity: therefore let Lebanon and Tabor, let Jerusalem and Galilee, know assuredly that God hath made our Lord the Lord of the Roman earth indeed, and that the influence of the Holy Ghost is Christ's continued life."

What if, later, when Christianity had ascended the throne of the Cæsars, Peter had stood on the Tiber, and had beheld philosophy, little by little, permeated

by Christianity? What if he had looked back on the
persecutions and martyrdoms which gave purity and
power to early Christianity, and which make her
record, even to your infidel Gibbon, venerable beyond comment? Could not Peter, there on the Tiber,
have said, looking on the Apennines and Vesuvius and
the Mediterranean, and on Egypt, "Let Rome and
the Tiber, let Alexandria and the Nile, know assuredly, since our Lord — who was, and is, and is to
come — hath shed forth this, that he is Lord"?

What if, later, Peter, standing on the Bosphorus,
when Rome had lost her footing on the Tiber, had
beheld the rushing in of the Turks to pulverize the
sunrise foot of old Rome; what if he had remembered the day, when, standing on two feet, Rome,
planting herself on both the Tiber and the Bosphorus, folded her arms, and looked at the North Star,
and proclaimed herself likely to be as eternal as that
stellar light; what if, remembering all that had come,
and all that had gone, he had beheld that Colossus
topple toward the West, smite itself into pieces on
the Alps, and fall in fragments on the Rhine, on the
Elbe, on the Oder, some pieces scattered across the
howling North Sea to the Thames, and to the sites of
Oxford and Cambridge, these fragments of old Rome,
built up in these places into universities which caused
at last the illumination which brought the Reformation; what if Peter, beholding thus the Greeks driven
toward the sunset, and old Rome becoming seed for
the Reformation, had stood on the Seine, on the Elbe,
on the Oder, and had witnessed the varied progress

of the ideas of Him who affirmed once that he had
many things yet to say, — might not Peter there,
side by side with Luther, have said once more, "He
hath shed forth this: therefore, let the Alps and the
Rhine and the Seine and the Elbe, the Thames and
the German Sea, know assuredly that this Gulf Current in human history, now two thousand years old,
is not an accident [applause]; that it means all it
expresses; for what God does, he from the first intends to do? He who has thus watched over the
cause of Christian truth, and has been breathing the
Holy Ghost upon the nations, hath shed forth this;
and, therefore, let Berlin and Paris and London, and
Oxford and Cambridge, know assuredly that God
hath made him Lord."

What if, later, when the tempest of persecution,
rising out of the sunrise, smote upon those universities, and blew the Mayflower across the sea, Peter
had taken position in that vessel, as its billowing,
bellying, bellowing sails fled across the great deep in
the icy breath of that time; and what if he had
seen, on the deck of that Mayflower, a few rush-lights taking their gleam from those universities,
themselves illumined by the fire that fell at Pentecost? What if Peter, afterward, standing on Plymouth Rock, had seen these rush-lights kindling
others, and a line of rush-lights, representing the
same illumination of the Holy Spirit, go out into our
wilderness, until they glass themselves in the Connecticut and in the Hudson, and in the eyes of the
wild beasts of the murmuring pines and hemlocks,

and in the eternal roar of Niagara, and in the Great Lakes, and in the Mississippi, and in the springs of the Sierras, and at last in the soft, hissing foam of the Pacific seas; what if, beholding these rush-lights thus carried across a continent by divine guidance, Peter had stood here, — would not the force of his word *therefore* have had new emphasis as he should have said, " He hath shed forth this: therefore, let Boston, let New York, let Chicago, let San Francisco, let the surf of the Bay of Fundy, let the waterfalls of the Yosemite, know assuredly that God hath made him Lord "?

But what if, when a tempest sprung out of the South, and these rush-lights were, I will not say extinguished, but all bent to the earth, and painfully tried, some of them blown out, he had beheld the lights, little by little, after the tempest had gone down, begin to be carried southward, and at last glass themselves in the steaming bayous and the Gulf? what if, although some had been extinguished forever, he had seen them shining on the breaking of the fetters of three million slaves? what if the churches, when the tempest ceases, grow brighter in their assertion of the value of their light, and are filling the land with its influence, and, if God continues to illumine them, will make the rush-lights glass themselves yet in all the streams, in all the springs, and in all the sprays on all the shores of all the land, — could not he, looking on such results in a territory greater than Rome ever ruled over, have said, " He hath shed forth this: therefore, let America know assuredly that God hath made him Lord "?

But what if, lastly, Peter had beheld a rush-light taken across the Pacific to the Sandwich Islands, and one to Japan, and one to China, and one to India, and had seen the soft rolling globe enswathed in all its zones by rush-lights bearing the very flames which fell at Pentecost, and beaten on, indeed, by persecution here and there, but not likely to be beaten on ever again as fiercely as they have been already; not likely to be blown out everywhere, even if they are in some places, and thus ensphering the globe so that it is not probable at all, under the law of the survival of the fittest, that they will be put out [applause], — could not Peter, then, looking on what God has done, and what he therefore intended to do; looking on the incontrovertible fact, that the islands of the sea and the continents have been coming to prefer Christian thought, and seem likely to remain under its influence, — could he not, while standing on scientific and biblical ground at once, have affirmed in the name both of science and of Scripture the transfiguring truth, " He hath shed forth this: therefore, let Asia on the Himalaya tops, let Europe in the Parthenon and Coliseum, let London's mystic roar, let the New World in her youthful vigor, let all the islands of the sea, know assuredly that the fittest has survived, and that the fittest will survive; and that God hath made him Lord who is fittest to be so"? All the seas, in all their waves, on all their shores, would answer to such an assertion, Hallelujah! So be it. The influences of the Holy Spirit are Christ's continued life. [Applause.]

XI.

FRAGMENTARINESS OF OUTLOOK UPON THE DIVINE NATURE.

THE SIXTY-NINTH LECTURE IN THE BOSTON MONDAY LECTURESHIP, DELIVERED IN TREMONT TEMPLE MARCH 12.

"Vox nostra quæ sit accipe.
Est Christus et Pater Deus:
Servi hujus ac testes sumus;
Extorque si potes fidem.

Tormenta, carcer, ungulæ
Stridensque flammis lamina
Atque ipsa pœnarum ultima;
Mors Christianis ludus est."

PRUD. PERISTEPH. HYMN, 5. 57.

"Deus autem et Pater Domini nostri Jesu Christi, et ipse Sempiternus Pontifex, Dei Filius Jesus Christus, ædificet vos in fide et veritate et in omni mansuetudine, . . . et det vobis sortem et partem inter sanctos suos." — POLYCARP, ad Phil., 12.

XI.

FRAGMENTARINESS OF OUTLOOK UPON THE DIVINE NATURE.

PRELUDE ON CURRENT EVENTS.

IN 1640 the whole population of New England was English, and consisted of only about four thousand families, or twenty thousand persons. Bancroft points out, that, after the first fifteen years following the landing on Plymouth Rock, there was no considerable addition from England. Your Palfrey shows, that, for one hundred and fifty years, the four thousand families multiplied in remarkable seclusion from other communities, and that it is only within the last fifty years that the foreigners have come. New England is changing the character of her population to such an extent, that we must now look for the descendants of those who crossed in the Mayflower, not so much on the Atlantic slope as in the Mississippi valley and on the Pacific coast. It is not true that New England is becoming New Ireland; but it is hardly epigrammatic to say that manufacturing New England is New Ireland already.

Perhaps we shall do well to remember, that, while the population of the manufacturing centres of New England is increasing with extraordinary rapidity, that of the agricultural and commercial districts is fluctuating, and, in many cases, on the decrease. The distinctions between the rich and poor are becoming wider in the manufacturing districts. This is partly the unavoidable result of the natural growth of the power of •capital. It is, in part, the consequence of the massing of men in cities as distinct from small towns. It is, to some extent, the effect of the organization of manufacturing industry in great corporations on the one side, and an operative population on the other. It is, in large measure, the result of the fact, that, in the manufacturing districts of New England, a vastly greater proportion of the population is now of foreign descent than fifty years ago. The two most typical things in the territory east of the Hudson are the college bell and the factory chimney. The first New England was a church; the second New England is to be a factory.

What is the worth of the church to the workingman?

Look at the seven cities on the Merrimack River. I often hang in imagination over that stream as the best emblem of the industrial life of Eastern New England. Child of the White Mountains and the Pemigewasset, the Merrimack rushes under the spindles of seven cities to the sea, — Concord, Manchester, Nashua, Lowell, Lawrence, Haverhill, Newburyport, — doing more work than any other river of its size in the world, and typical more and more of the future into which our Atlantic New-England slope is drifting. These seven cities have in the aggregate, in the last twenty years, more than doubled in wealth and population. Romish cathedral churches are rising in our manufacturing centres, and are not likely to be empty. But, under the voluntary system, many of our Protestant churches are looked upon by a portion of the operatives as close corporations. When a church is not mossy, it is aristocratic, our workingmen too often think; and so our floating, unchurched populations are coming to be very large in our factory centres.

If I were a working-man, I presume I should want fair play between employers and employed. I think I should care for my children, and desire to have a better place for them than Old England gives the very youngest at the factory-wheel. It seems almost incredible, that some of the acutest members of our Protestant factory-population are falling into neglect of the church, when it is certain that only by the diffusion of conscientiousness among the laboring-classes can co-operation ever succeed; and that conscientiousness will not be diffused without the use of means which the Church herself employs none too thoroughly, but which no other organization pretends to employ at all as a permanent system for the culture of society. Can co-operation ever succeed, unless there are large numbers of honest men in society?

How are these to be made? In commerce you want a revival of business. You want, therefore, a revival of undefiled religion. How are you to have that, if you are to neglect, I will not say this or that branch of the church, but the church as a whole? If you are to shut the doors of God's house on the Sabbath, how are you to be sure that diffusion of conscientiousness will come? Why do not working-men see the great impropriety of their neglecting the church, and that the church is made up of men, many of whom have risen from the bench of the shoemaker, or from the wheel of the operative? Our New-England society is not divided into hereditary and fixed classes. We must look on our churches as the work of the people; and it is not American for a portion of our New-England population to regard our churches as aristocratic machines. Perhaps some of them are; I am not defending the whole list of them; but most of them, I think ninety out of a hundred, are eager to be of service in the diffusion of conscientiousness, and all culture and comfort, among the factory population, and in the beating down of all the walls of division between the workmen and their employers. [Applause.]

You want arbitration committees; you want fair consultation between capital and labor? Bring your whole population together once a week in the church, where all class-walls are, or ought to be, broken down. [Applause.] I am not speaking of all the churches; for God has not granted to all men the capacity to burst asunder the silken bonds of luxury:

he has to some men, and to some who are very wealthy. But the most of our churches in New England were built by the people, and come from the hearts of the average population; and it is absolutely suicidal for the working-man to let his children grow up without the religious culture of the church. [Applause.]

Have you ever heard that the Sabbath schools have been greatly improved in the last fifty years? There is a liberal denomination which lately has been issuing Sabbath-school volumes with questions about the relations between religion and science. I thank God for that step in advance. Let it be understood that the Sabbath school is now a better thing than it used to be, and that you cannot let your children stay out of it without putting them behind other children. Do you wish to have that spirit of good sense pervade the community which you would like to find in the arbitration board? You will never have it, unless you take possession of the church and of the ministry. The latter are rather a numerous and well-educated class, and they have much opportunity to study public questions: why cannot you win them to your side? [Applause.] There is a strategic act for workingmen to do on the Merrimack! [Applause.]

When you and I are no longer in the world, the supreme question in New-England civilization will be how to make Plymouth Rock the corner-stone of a factory. [Applause.] Do not say that I am uttering any thing irreverent, when I speak of that sacred spot on the shore yonder as fit to be the beginning of the newest New England, as it was of the earliest. Plymouth Rock was the corner-stone of the first New England: shall it be the corner-stone of the second? Where are the builders that shall place that jagged and fundamental rock in line with the other stones of the wall? Shall we hew the factory to make it fit Plymouth Rock, or Plymouth Rock to fit the factory? God send us no future into which Plymouth Rock cannot be built unhewn! [Applause.] You think it is a very unpoetic, prosaic fact, that New England is to be a factory. Goethe, our modern philosopher and poet, used to say the sound of spindles in Manchester was the most poetic sound of this century. Not every man has Goethe's ears. He foresaw the time when a greater proportion than now of the population of the world will be in cities, and when the most numerous inhabitants in cities will be of the operative class. Thomas Carlyle says somewhere, "Have you ever listened to the awakening of Manchester in Old England at half-past five by the clock? ten thousand times ten thousand looms and spindles all set moving there, like the broom of an Atlantic tide. It is, if you think of it, sublime as Niagara, or more so." Sometimes I have repeated to myself these words when awaking in the gray morning on Beacon Hill, as I have listened to the factory bells, and allowed imagination to move up the Merrimack, past Newburyport, Haverhill, and Lawrence and Lowell, and Manchester and Concord, and to see the crowds of the operative class coming out in streams in the early dawn. It is sublime, and it is to be more and more sublime as the years pass? But only the church, captured by the working-men, and able to capture the working-men in return, can prevent in our free society, when once New England is crowded with manufacturing centres, those collisions between capital and labor which have arisen in the Old World. [Applause.] You never can bridge the chasm between capital and labor here by a kid glove. [Applause.] You never can bridge it with the bayonet. [Applause.] In the Old World it has been bridged by the bayonet on the continent and by the kid glove in England; but in New England the only bridge that will cross that chasm is popular, scientific, aggressive, deadly Christianity, laid on the buttresses of the Sabbaths and the common schools. [Applause.]

THE LECTURE.

The River Rhine is a majestic stream, until, in the Netherlands of the North Sea shore, it divides into shallows and swamps and steaming oozes. Man's adoration of God is a majestic stream, until, in the Netherlands of religious experience, it divides among three Gods, or among many Gods, and so becomes a collection of shallows and swamps and steaming oozes. Out of these North Sea hollow lands, wherever they have existed in any age of the moral experience of the race, there has invariably arisen a vapor obscuring the wide, undivided azure, and even the near landscapes of natural truth. Give me the Christian and the scientific surety of the unity of the Divine Nature, and let my whole soul flow toward one God; let me not worship three separate wills, three separate consciences, three separate sets of affections, but one Will, one Conscience, one Heart, which was, and is, and is to come; and so long as the Alps of thought feed me with their cool, impetuous, crystalline streams, I shall be like the Rhine, deep enough in the current of my adoring affections to drive out the drift-wood and bowlders in the stream, and not permit them to accumulate, and form islands to divide the river into shallows and oozes. Let me move toward God, one in nature outside of the soul, one in Christ revealed in history, one as tangible to the conscience in the intuitions. Let me feel that all these subsistences are one Substance; and it may be that the Rhine of the human affections, turned thus toward God as one Will, one Heart, and one Conscience, will be majestic enough to float fleets both for peace and for war [applause]; and will go out into the ocean at last, not as a set of befogged shallows and oozes, but as the Amazon goes out, an undivided river into an undivided ocean, a thousand flashing leagues caught up into infinite times ten thousand flashing leagues, the interspheriug of wave with wave in every case, the interspersing of a portion of the finite personality with the Infinite Personality, one, invisible, omnipotent, omnipresent, eternal, the same yesterday, to-day, and forever, holy, holy, holy, Father, Son, and Holy Ghost.

For one, I had rather, my friends, go back to the Bosphorus, where I stood a few months ago, and worship with that emperor who lately slit his veins, and went hence by suicide, than to be in name only an orthodox believer, or in theory to hold that there is but one God, but in imagination to worship three Gods. I am orthodox, I hope; but my first concern, is to be straightforward. I purpose to be straightforward, even if I must be orthodox. [Applause.] Revere the orthodoxy of straightforwardness; and when that justifies you in doing so, but only then, revere the straightforwardness of orthodoxy. [Applause.] Mahometan Paganism yonder contains one great truth, — the Divine Unity; and I never touch this majestic theme of the Divine Triunity without remembering what that single truth, as I heard it uttered on the Bosphorus, did for me when I knelt there once in a mosque with the emperor and with the peasants, with the highest officers of state and with the artisans, and saw them all bow down, and bring their foreheads to the mats of the temple, and heard them call out, from the highest to the lowest, as they prostrated themselves, "Allah el akbar!" "God is one, and God is great." So, prostrating themselves, they three times called out, "Allah el akbar!" and then remained silent, until I felt that this one truth had in it a transfiguration. I affirm that I had rather go back to that shore of the azure water which connects the Black Sea with the Mediterranean, and, omitting the leprosy of Mahometanism, take for my religion pure Theism, than to hold that there are three Gods with three wills, three sets of affections, three intellects, three consciences, and thus to deny the assurances of both scriptural and scientific truth, and make of myself the beginning of a polytheist, although calling myself orthodox.

At what should we arrive, however, if we should adopt the bare idea of the Divine Unity without taking also that of the Triunity? Should we thus be faithful to the scientific method? Should we thus be looking at all the facts? Should we obtain by this method the richest conception of God, or should we see from such a point of view only a fragment of that portion of his nature which man may apprehend?

Theodore Parker taught God's Immanence in mind and matter, and it is amazing that he thought this truth a new one. If you are of my opinion, you will reverence that one portion of his far from original teaching; for it is at once a scientific and a Christian certainty, that, wherever God acts, there he is. The Bridgewater Treatises affirm this truth with more emphasis than Parker ever laid upon it. The one chord which he struck in theology to which all hearts vibrate was the certainty of the Divine Immanence in matter and mind; and this one certainty was the secret of any power he had in distinctively religious endeavor. Men, he said, have a conscience; and in that conscience the moral law is revealed; and that moral law reveals a Holy Person.

Your Helmholtz and Wundt, and Beale and

Carpenter, and Herschel and Faraday, and Darwin and Agassiz, as well as your Lotze and Kant and Leibnitz, and your St. Chrysostom, and Jeremy Taylor, and Archbishop Butler, all unite with Plato and Aristotle, and David and Isaiah, in asserting the Divine Personal Immanence in matter and mind. There is no cloud at this moment shot through by the noon so completely saturated by light as all mind and matter are by the Divine Immanence; that is to say, by this invisible, incomprehensible Personality which the moral law reveals.

But, granting the fact of the Divine Personal immanence in matter and mind, to what results must a rigid use of the scientific method bring us on the theme of the Triunity of the Divine Nature? I know of no question on this topic fairer or more fruitful than this.

1. Since a Personal God is immanent in all matter and mind, it follows, that, in all nature outside the soul, we look into God's face.

2. For the same reason, it is incontrovertible, that in the soul we call Christ, and in his influence in history, we look into God's face.

3. For the same reason, it is certain, that, in the intuitions of conscience, we look into God's face.

4. *These three spheres of his self-manifestation embrace all of God that can be known to man.*

5. *In each of these spheres of the self-manifestation of the Divine Nature, something is shown which is not shown with equal clearness in either of the other spheres. In each of them, the Ineffable Immanent Person says something new.*

6. In external nature he appears chiefly as Creator; in Christ chiefly as Redeemer; in conscience chiefly as Sanctifier.

7. These are all facts scientifically known.

8. *A scientific scheme of religious thought must look at all the facts.*

9. *When all the facts known to man are taken into view, a Trinity of Divine Manifestations is, therefore, scientifically demonstrable.*

10. *But, according to the admitted proposition that a Personal God is immanent in all matter and mind, he reveals himself in each of these manifestations as a Person, and yet as one.*

11. *A Personal Triunity, of which Creator, Redeemer, and Sanctifier are but other names, is therefore scientifically known to exist.*

12. This is the Trinity which Christianity calls Father, Son, and Holy Ghost, and of all parts of whose undivided glory it inculcates adoration in the name of what God is, and of what he has done, and of what man needs,

All these propositions you will grant me, except the second ; but you cannot deny that, without throwing away your own admission that a Personal God is immanent in all matter and mind.

Even Rousseau could say that Socrates died like a man, but the Founder of Christianity like a God. Carlyle affirms that Voltaire's attacks on Christianity are a battering-ram, swinging in the wrong direction. Who doubts, that, at the head of the effect we call Christianity, there was an adequate

Cause, or a Person? and who can deny, that, in the soul of that Person, God spake to man as never before or since? Scholarship has outgrown the old forms of historical doubt; and historical science now admits, that, whether we say Christ possessed proper Deity or not, he assuredly has been the chief religious teacher of the race. But that fact means more than much, if looked at on all sides. Keep in mind here that glimpse of the world history on which we were gazing when last we parted from this Temple.

Napoleon at St. Helena said that something mysterious exists in universal history in its relation to Christianity. "Can you tell me who Jesus Christ was?" said this Italian, greater than Cæsar, and as free from partisan religious prejudices. The question was declined by Bertrand; and Napoleon proceeded, "Well, then, I will tell you." I am reading now from a passage authorized by three of Napoleon's biographers, and freely accepted by European scholars as an authoritative statement of his conversation in exile. (See LIDDON's *Bampton Lectures*, Eng. ed., p. 148, for a full list of authorities for this extract.) "Alexander, Cæsar, Charlemagne, and I myself have founded great empires; but upon what did these creations of our genius depend? Upon force. Jesus alone founded his empire upon love; and to this very day millions would die for him. . . . I think I understand something of human nature; and I tell you all these were men, and I am a man. No other is like him: Jesus Christ was more than a man. I have inspired multitudes with such an enthusiastic devotion, that they would have died for me: but, to do this, it was necessary that I should be *visibly* present with the electric influence of my looks, of my words, of my voice. When I saw men, and spoke with them, I lighted up the flame of self-devotion in their hearts. . . . Christ alone has succeeded in so raising the mind of man toward the Unseen, that it becomes insensible to the barriers of time and space. Across a chasm of eighteen hundred years Jesus Christ makes a demand which is beyond all others difficult to satisfy. He asks for that which a philosopher may often seek in vain at the hands of his friends, or a father of his children, or a bride of her spouse, or a man of his brother. He asks for the human heart; he will have it entirely to himself; he demands it unconditionally, and forthwith his demand is granted. Wonderful! In defiance of time and space, the soul of man, with all its powers and faculties, becomes an annexation to the empire of Christ. *All who sincerely believe in him experience that remarkable supernatural love towards him. This phenomenon is unaccountable; it is altogether beyond the scope of man's creative powers. Time, the great destroyer, is powerless to extinguish this sacred flame: time can neither exhaust its strength, nor put a limit to its range. This is what strikes me most: I have often thought of it. This it is which proves to me quite convincingly the divinity of Jesus Christ.*" [Applause.]

It is beyond all controversy, that precisely this central thought of Christianity which convinced

Napoleon was what most struck the ancient Roman philosophers. Christ's continued life in the Holy Spirit, was that heard of in the first centuries? Why, I open an ancient book, written in opposition to Christianity, and cited by Arnobius, and I read, " Our gods are not displeased with you Christians for worshipping the Almighty God; but you maintain the Deity of one who was put to death on the cross; you believe him to be yet alive (*et superesse adhuc creditis*), and you adore him with daily supplications" (ARNOBIUS, *adv. Gentes*, i. 36). Pliny's letter to Trajan implies all this, but is so celebrated, that I need not recite its majestic facts here.

Men showed me at Rome, in the Kircherian Museum, a square foot of the plaster of a wall of a palace, not many years ago uncovered on the Palatine Hill. On the poor clay was traced a cross bearing a human figure with a brute's head. The figure was nailed to the cross ; and before it a soldier was represented kneeling, and extending his hands, in the Greek posture of devotion. Underneath all was scratched in rude lettering in Greek, " *Alexamenos adores his God.*" That representation of the central thought of Christianity was made in a jeering moment by some rude soldier in the days of Caracalla; but it blazes there now in Rome, the most majestic monument of its age in the world. (See LIDDON, *Bampton Lectures*, p. 396.)

You believe *your* Lord is yet alive? You adore him? All the history of the early persecutions of Christianity accords with the import of this Kircherian symbol. Listen to the last words of the martyrs through all the first five centuries of Christianity. They are these, and such as these: "O Lord God of heaven and earth, Jesu Christ, to thee do I bend my neck by way of sacrifice; O Thou who abidest forever." These were the words of Felix, an African bishop, condemned to death at Venusium. (See for a multitude of similar instances RUINART's celebrated work, *Acta Martyrum Sincera*, edition Veronæ.) "O Lord Jesu Christ, Thou Maker of heaven and earth, give peace unto thy Church." So spoke Theodotus of Ancyra in the extremity of torture. (*Ibid.*, p. 303.)

Poor Blandina, there at Lyons in the year 177, you remember how they roasted her, frail girl, on the red-hot iron chair; put her in a net and exposed her to the horns of oxen; whirled her in instruments of torture until her senses were lost, and then plunged her into flames; and day after day did that, while she apparently experienced little pain, calling out at every interval when her strength came back, "I am a Christian: there is no evil done among us." And so she passed hence, but speaks to us as one yet living. (See EUSEBIUS, v. 1–3, for a contemporary account of Blandina in a letter written from the churches of Lyons and Vienne to those of Asia Minor.) She "hastened to Christ," says an account written by eye-witnesses of her sufferings; and they send " to those having the same faith and hope," "Peace, and grace, and glory from God the Father, and Christ Jesus, our Lord." Multitudes and multitudes, a great army of martyrs, passed out of the world, believing that the influence of the Holy Spirit was Christ's continued life; and, if there is any thing mysterious in history, Napoleon had his eye upon it when he asked what it is that makes the martyrs in every age painless when on the bosom of their spouse.

There was a God in Christ, whether you regard him as divine or not; and that was one revelation of God which was made, and is now making, in this incontrovertible fact of his earthly influence, which Napoleon thought utterly inexplicable on merely human lines of cause and effect. But in conscience there is a God. In the moral intuitions of the soul we look into God's face. Assuredly, even if you and I were not to have, a better age will have, a religious science that will take into view all these facts. There is a God in external nature; there is a God in Christ; there is a God in the intuitions of the human spirit: and if I could not have any other Trinity than that, although I do not believe that to be the best, I would have that, for I want all the truth I can reach. I, therefore, will look on God as manifesting himself in external nature, and in our intuitions, and in history as influenced by his spirit; and my God will be thus revealed to me with more fulness than he could be if I had only one of these three personal revelations of himself. In each of them he says what he does not say elsewhere. Science must be hungry to hear all that all facts say.

God is a person in each one of these revelations.

He is a person in the strict sense, as seen in external nature. As seen in our Lord, he is a person in the strict sense. As revealed in the moral law, he is a person in the strict sense. *But there are not three persons: he is one person in the strict sense; for natural law is a unit in the universe, and reveals but one will.* Three revelations of God are all one person, although in each revelation he is a person. Now, is that mystical? or does that straightforward use of the scientific method give a richer view of human history, a richer view of the human soul, a richer view of external nature, than mere deism, or theism, or materialism, or pantheism, however fortified by modern science, can present to you?

Thus far, gentlemen, I have asked you to notice only what is involved in Theodore Parker's admission that a personal God is immanent in all matter and mind. On this point, as on so many others, Theodore Parker failed to carry out consistently his own principles, and fell into error not so much through a wrong direction as through haste, and incompleteness of research. If, my friends, I must at this point, to save time, drop analytical discussion, and give personal conviction, let me say that Theodore Parker's scheme of thought, melodious as that one feebly-struck note of the Divine Immanence in mind and matter is, compares to me with Christianity as water compares with wine. Tennyson makes one of his characters say to another,

"All thy passions matched with mine
Are as moonlight unto sunlight,
And as water unto wine."

So I aver, in the name of the precision of the scientific method, that any scheme of thought not Christian, as matched with Christianity, and tested fairly by intuition, instinct, syllogism, and ages of experiment, is as moonlight matched with sunlight, or as water matched with wine.

I want supremely such a view of religious truth as shall set me at rest about my irreversible record of sin. [Applause.] I want such a view of God as shall present him as an atoning God, on whom I cannot look without the regeneration of my own nature through gratitude, and on whom I can look, and yet, for his sake, be at peace.

Why do the ages cling to the doctrines of the Trinity? Perhaps their wants have been much like yours and mine. Is the truth of the Divine Trinity dear to us, because it is a fine piece of philosophical speculation? Ah, gentlemen, you know life too well to think that eighteen centuries have offered up their martyrdoms, and the personal careers, which, not ending at the stake, have been bound to the stake perhaps through the better part of the time from birth to death, and that these ages have had nothing more than philosophy behind them. *Great human organic wants are revealed by the reception the world has given to the deepest religious truths. We know we are going hence. We wish to go hence in peace. We want a religion that can wash Lady Macbeth's red right hand. We need to know that an atonement has been provided, such that we may look on all God's attributes, and then in his merit, not in our own, be at peace* here and in that Unseen Holy into which it is scientifically sure that all men haste.

Religious science never teaches that personal demerit is or can be transferred from an individual, finite personality to God. That is a ghastly error which has been charged to Christianity in every age, and nowhere more audaciously or inexcusably than in this city. [Applause.] It is one of the most monstrous of misconceptions, one of the most unphilosophical of all the hideous caricatures set up by Theodore Parker before the public gaze, that Christianity teaches that personal demerit or blame-worthiness may be taken off one soul, and put upon another, and that one an innocent being. We hold nothing of the sort; but we have been taught that there is revealed in Christianity a view of God which represents him as substituting chastisement for punishment, and as thus making possible the peace of all who are loyal to him; and this has been the regenerating influence which has brought the human spirit to the highest summits it has ever attained; so that, both by ages of experience and by philosophy, we know that this central portion of the Christian scheme of thought is adapted to man's deepest wants. [Applause.]

If you deny the doctrine of the Trinity, you must deny the whole central portion of this crowned system of truth, in all its philosophical glory and in all its prolonged and multiplex breadth of power in human experience. There was nothing so touching, when Professor Huntington of Harvard University yonder turned toward the doctrine of the Trinity, as his proclamation of the "life, comfort, and salvation" which burst upon his vastly enlarged horizon as he attained at once the scientific, the biblical, and the only historically radiant point of view. (See HUNTINGTON, ARCHBISHOP, *Christian Believing and Living.*)

Only an undiluted Christianity gives such a view of God, that we can be true to the scientific method, and yet at peace with all his attributes.

Gentlemen, you will not soon drive out of human nature the desire to go hence in peace. You will not soon remove from human nature the feeling it has exhibited in every age, that peace does not come even when we reform. You will not soon change the natural operations of conscience. You will not soon cause the past to be reversible. You, therefore, will not soon make the atonement any thing other than a desire of all nations. But, until you have done all these things, there will be life, there will be a wholly natural and abounding vitality, in that exhibition of God's nature to man, which represents him as an atoning God, and as a person who was, and is, and is to be with us, because one with Him who made heaven and earth, and with Him who speaks in conscience at this hour, and who, from eternity to eternity, is our Saviour and our Lord.

But, next, I want in my view of religion something that will bring me into harmony with all exact research. I want no mysticism, no mediævalism, no doctrine supported simply by the schools, or of doubtful worth under the microscope and the scalpel.

I find it beyond controversy, as Theodore Parker held, that a Personal God is immanent in matter and mind. It is beyond all debate that there is a Holy Person revealed by the moral law. I want a God who shall be one in history, in external nature, and in my intuitions; and I turn to Christianity, and I find a breadth of outlook more than equal to the loftiest philosophical demand. I read that He who is the light that lighteth every man that cometh into the world, that is, the Personal God who is revealed in conscience, is also He whose light shone in the darkness, and the darkness comprehended it not; and who was in the world which was made by him, and the world knew him not. He who speaketh in the still small voice is he who spoke, and who yet speaks, as never man spoke. If we do not force upon the Scriptures our own narrowness of thought, we find that science and Scripture are agreed, for both make God perfect and one; and, according to the Scriptures, the Holy Spirit is Christ's continued life.

What are the great proofs in Scripture that God is presented to us as triunity in unity? What are the great biblical proofs that God is triune? What are a few of the tremorless bases of conviction that the Trinity is taught in the New Testament? I hold, my friends, that it is a cheap reply to the assertion that the Trinity is taught in the New Testament, to say that the word is not there. The word "Christianity" is not there; the word "Deity" is not there; the word "humanity" is not there. The question is, whether it is not taught in the New Testament that God is one. You say, Yes. If it be taught in the New Testament that God is one, and that each of the three subsistences is God, the Trinity is taught there implicitly, though not explicitly. After ages of debate, you know what nine out of ten of the devoutest and acutest think the New Testament teaches in the baptismal formula and the apostolical benediction, two incisive biblical summaries of Christian truth. The direction to the apostles as to baptism was, "Baptize all nations in the name of the Father, Son, and Holy Ghost," a Triune Name, no distinction being made between these three. So, too, the benediction was pronounced in the Triune Name: "May the love of God, the grace of the Lord Jesus Christ, and the communion of the Holy Ghost, be with you." You have been told that Neander says that there is not a passage in the New Testament which asserts the doctrine of the Trinity explicitly; and Neander does say so: but he says a great deal more; namely, that the whole New Testament contains the doctrine implicitly. [Applause.]

"In the doctrine of the Trinity," he writes, "God becomes known as Creator, Redeemer, and Sanctifier, in which threefold relation the whole Christian knowledge of God is completely announced. Accordingly all is herein embraced by the apostle Paul, when, in pronouncing the benediction, he sums up all in the formula, the grace of the Lord Jesus Christ, the love of God, and the communion of the Holy Spirit. God as the living God, the God of mankind, and the

God of the church, can be truly known in this way only. This shape of Theism presents the perfect mean between the wholly extra-mundane God of deism and the God brought down into, and confounded with, the world of pantheism. This mode of the knowledge of God belongs to the peculiar science of Theism and the Theocracy" (NEANDER, *Hist. of the Chr. Rel. and Ch., Torrey's trans.* i. 572).

As many windows, gentlemen, as there are facts, let us use when we gaze on religious truths. Your mere theism shuts me up to one window. You will not let me look on all quarters of the sky. You shut your eyes to the light when you will not recognize what Napoleon saw in history. *I want no pulpit that is not built on rendered reasons; but I must be allowed to find reasons wherever they exist, whether the heavens stand or fall.*

Let research, with the four tests of intuition, instinct, experiment, and syllogism, have free course, and I am content. For fear that your conclusions may be a little broader than you like, you will not fail to gaze on the evidence which convinces Neander that the outcome of all looking into the Scriptures and into mere reason must be a belief in a Creator, in a Redeemer, and in a Sanctifier, the three one God, personal, omnipresent, and in conscience tangible.

When I thus use all my light, I am delivered from materialism; when I thus look on God, I am delivered from pantheism.

Whoever searches the Bible in the spirit of those

who wrote it, and of the martyrs, will be kept free from an utterly unscientific narrowness which feels that God in Christ *was* rather than that He *is*. We are not abreast of our privileges when we live always in Judæa. [Applause.] The Scriptures are a map of the universe, and not of Palestine merely. If we are full of their spirit, the wings of philosophy will tire us only by their tardiness, and narrow range of flight.

There are in all ages, and particularly in this age of special studies, the most terrific dangers in a fragmentary view of God. I want this doctrine of the Trinity to save me from fragmentariness of outlook upon the Divine Nature. I will not allow myself to see God merely in my intuitions, and shut up the windows of external nature and of history; for thus I may easily drop down into pantheistic individualism, which, with supreme felicity of speech, your brave, broad, and massive Thomas Hill calls Egotheism. [Applause.] (See HILL, ex-president of Harvard University, *The Theology of the Sciences*, 1877.)

Neander says that the doctrine of the Trinity implies that of the Theocracy, or of a government of God in the universe and in national history. Remember, gentlemen, that our fathers came here avowedly to found a Theocracy. What did that mean? A state of which natural law and revelation together, shining under, in, and about legislation, should be the masters; a state where what can be known of God by reason on the one side, and revelation on the other, should lock its two hands around the neck of all vice, and throttle whatever would throttle the

Christian well-being of the poorest or the highest, and should thus build up in history a state fit to be called at once natural and God's own. When the Jesuits came to the mouth of the St. Lawrence, they intended to found a Theocracy. The great dream that lay behind Milton's and Cromwell's and Hampden's thoughts and deeds was, that human legislation should be a close copy of the divine and natural law. At the point of view to which exact research has now brought us, we must assert that the fact of the Divine Immanence in matter and mind makes the world and nations a Theocracy; and that politics and social life, no less than philosophy, must beware of fragmentary outlooks on the Divine Nature. Richter said, "He who was the Holiest among the mighty, and the Mightiest among the holy, has, with his pierced hand, lifted heathenism off its hinges, and turned the dolorous and accursed centuries into new channels, and now governs the ages." History, the illuminated garment of God; the church, Christ's Temple,—did you ever hear of the former in the name of science, or of the latter in the name of Christianity? But to your Titanic Richter the two are one. De Tocqueville affirms anxiously that men never so much need to be theocratic as when they are the most democratic. Democracy will save itself by turning into a Theocracy, or ruin itself by not doing so. [Applause.]

Transfigure society with Richter's thought. Saturate the centuries with the certainty of the Divine Personal Immanence in matter and mind. Do this, and, in the name of science itself, the laboring ages will slowly learn, not merely admiration, but adoration, of one God, incontrovertibly known in external nature, history, and conscience as Creator, as Redeemer, as Sanctifier. When they touch the hem of the garment of a personal God thus apprehended, and never till then, will they be healed of the measureless evils arising from fragmentariness of outlook upon the Divine Nature. Let the forehead of science, in the name of Christianity, bow down upon the moral law as the beloved disciple did upon our Lord's bosom. Let Richter lead; and a time will come when all clear thought, all political action, all individual growth, will call out: Glory be to God revealed in external nature; glory be to God revealed in Christ and the church; glory be to God revealed in Conscience! To this secular voice the church will answer, in words which have already led eighteen centuries, and science will add at last her momentous acclaim; Glory be to the Father, and to the Son, and to the Holy Ghost; as it was in the beginning, is now, and ever shall be, world without end. [Applause.]

THE INDEPENDENT
FOR 1878

will have to be a very good paper to satisfy the thousands of readers who have become familiar with its good qualities in the past. Some of them have taken it for nearly thirty years, and know how carefully its standard of excellence is maintained. But we want, if we can, to make it so much better than ever before, that a new army of subscribers will come to know and prize it. Next year we shall print no serial story, and so will be able to give more attention to our numerous and full Editorial Departments, to our great feature of Contributed Articles by famous American and European writers, and to the several enterprises mentioned below.

REV. JOSEPH COOK'S LECTURES

in Tremont Temple, Boston, attracted great attention as printed in THE INDEPENDENT last winter; and their publication will be resumed immediately upon the commencement of the current course. They will be faithfully reported in full, and will be printed after a careful revision by the author. Mr. Cook has proved to be a foeman worthy of the steel of the scientists, whom he has met and defeated on their own ground. The earnest defender of the good old evangelical doctrines, he is entirely familiar with the very latest forms and phases of modern unbelief, which he attacks with a keen blade. His lectures are an armory of Christian defence and attack, and will attract even wider attention this year than last.

THE YALE LECTURES ON PREACHING,

which every minister and layman ought to read, will be delivered this year by one of the most noted of English Congregationalists, the Rev. R. W. Dale, editor of *The Congregationalist*, of London. Mr. Dale's lectures will be heard and read with great interest, and will be fully reported in THE INDEPENDENT. He is a scholar and an orator; and his lectures, coming from an English divine, will doubtless impart new suggestions to our pulpit-teachers, especially as Mr. Dale is a man of great force and rhetorical power. These lectures will begin the latter part of October.

SERMONS

by eminent divines of all denominations will continue to be printed regularly through the year. They have been very popular during the past twelve months; and the American Pulpit is now adequately represented only in THE INDEPENDENT.

THE REGULAR DEPARTMENTS

will all be continued. They are of great variety, and contain the newest information on all current topics. The Editorials and Editorial Notes frankly and ably discuss the most important religious, political, and social subjects. The Religious News columns, considerably enlarged this year, will continue to give a complete and impartial record of the doings of all the denominations, at home and abroad. The Ministerial Register supplements the Religious News by its list of clerical changes and deaths. The Sunday-school columns will be a scholars' and teachers' hand-book to the International Lessons, and will chronicle the news in that important field. The Book Reviews will give an impartial account of all the new books, and there will also be a full record of Literary News. Scientific Progress, Missionary News, Personal and Art Gossip, Educational Intelligence, Agricultural Interests, Commercial, Financial, and Insurance subjects, will all have their regular weekly columns. These departments are famous because they are trustworthy.

CONTRIBUTED ARTICLES

for old and young will be furnished by almost all our leading poets and prose-writers.

OUR NEW PREMIUM

is one of the most attractive we have ever issued, being the Rev. Joseph Cook's valuable new volumes, entitled "Biology" and "Transcendentalism," embodying in a revised and perfected form the author's remarkable Monday Lectures. Each volume is published by James R. Osgood & Co. of Boston, in handsome typography and binding; and is accompanied by several colored illustrations. Notwithstanding the expense of the premium, — the costliest we have ever offered, — we will mail a copy of either volume, postpaid, to every Subscriber to THE INDEPENDENT, New or Old, who remits us Three Dollars for one year, in advance, and indicates which volume he desires; or any Subscriber may remit Five Dollars and Fifty Cents, and we will send him THE INDEPENDENT for two years, and both volumes, postage prepaid, — thus giving a complete and permanently valuable work on the important questions at issue between science and religion. The first volume, on "Biology," is now ready for delivery; and the second, "Transcendentalism," we shall be able to forward very soon. They are just the right sort of reading for winter evenings, and Subscribers should remit at once. The books will be forwarded as fast as the names are received.

We also offer the following premiums, any one of which will be sent, if asked for, with one year's subscription in advance: —

Any one volume of the Household Edition of Charles Dickens's Works, bound in Cloth, with 16 Illustrations each, by SOL EYTINGE.

FOR FIFTEEN SUBSCRIBERS we will send DICKENS COMPLETE.

Moody and Sankey's " Gospel Hymns and Sacred Songs No. 2."
" Lincoln and his Cabinet; or, First Reading of the Emancipation Proclamation." Fine Large Steel Engraving. By RITCHIE. Size 26x36.
" Authors of the United States." Fine Large Steel Engraving. 44 Portraits. Size 24x38½. By RITCHIE.
" Charles Sumner." Fine Steel Engraving. By RITCHIE.
" Grant or Wilson." Fine Steel Engravings. By RITCHIE.
" Edwin M. Stanton." Fine Steel Engraving. By RITCHIE.
The " Inner Life of Abraham Lincoln." By FRANK B. CARPENTER. Bound in Cloth. 360 pages.

It gives a better insight into his "inner life" than can be found elsewhere, and is altogether one of the most fascinating, instructive, and useful books of the kind ever published.

SUBSCRIPTION $3.00 PER ANNUM, IN ADVANCE.

Specimen-copies of THE INDEPENDENT sent free.

Address   **THE INDEPENDENT,**
P. O. Box 2787.   **NEW YORK CITY.**